Endorsements

"The tea-time expert has done it a~~gain.~~ ~~~~ ~~~~ ~~~~ y, recipes, and personal insights into the wonderful world of tea. A must for all *Downton Abbey* Fans."

Linda Evans Shepherd, Best Selling Author, Award Winning Speaker, President of Right to the Heart, Advanced Writers and Speakers Association, and Publisher of Leading Hearts Magazine.

"Penelope's knowledge of the propriety of the ceremony of English tea is a joy to experience. Her interest and knowledge of my Great Grandmother, Margaret Brown, is enhanced by her enthusiasm for the Edwardian era. This wonderful book is a must for anyone who loves history, tea, *Downton Abbey* or the Titanic."

Helen Benziger, great-granddaughter of The Unsinkable Molly Brown.

"Steeped in God's word, Lady Penelope will quiet your spirit and warm your heart…like a good cup of tea. Her stories of Royalty and tea time are fabulous, plus some wonderful insights into *Downton Abbey*. Wonderful recipes! Don't miss it!"

-Rose Sweet, Author, Inspirational Speaker and Motivator
The Catholic's Divorce Survival Guide", "Dear God, Send Me a Soul Mate" and "A Woman's Guide to Healing the Heartbreak of Divorce"

"Passion for tea, passion for Jesus. Put the two together and what do you have? Lady Penelope, the Queen of Tea shares how you can refresh the souls of others with simple and elegant hospitality. Delight as she shares from her heart, real life tea parties and recipes fit for a King. A must have book for any history or tea lover with a heart for hospitality."

-Allison Bottke, bestselling author of *God Allows U-Turns book series, Setting Boundaries Books,* speaker and entrepreneur

"She knows tea! A best-selling author and expert on all things tea, Penelope practices what she preaches. She has expertly combined history with practical insights from the *Downton Abbey* sensation and on the Titanic with fabulous award-winning recipes. A must have for all *Downton Abbey* fans."

Jessica Avery, owner The House of Commons Tea Room, Denver, Colorado

The Art of Afternoon Tea: From the Era of Downton Abbey and the Titanic

• • •

Penelope M. Carlevato

The Art of Afternoon Tea:
From the Era of Downton Abbey and the Titanic

Additional Books by Penelope M. Carlevato

Tea on the Titanic
First Class Etiquette

In memory of my dear tea friend, Jessie Klingler.

Acknowledgments

• • •

A BOOK IS NEVER THE product of one person…it takes a village to get it done! Acknowledging those who have assisted me in the creation of this book is such a privilege. God gives us special people along the way who help make writing books a joy. My English mother, Thelma Barrett Schwarting, was my mentor and teacher in all things tea. She encouraged me every step of the way and gave me a rich legacy in every area of my life. Enormous thanks to my husband, Norm, for his patience, encouragement, and expert technical advise (which I don't always take). Thanks to Rick Marschall, author, editor, historian, and political cartoonist for his example of grace and expertise in editing and permission to use the wonderful Gibson Girl images. My granddaughters, Kate Carlevato, for special editing help, and Nicole Klingler, for recipe collecting and testing. A special thank you to friends Alan and Lyn Dines, who shared their royal adventure at Buckingham Palace, George Mynatt for sharing his "Mr. Carson" experience, and my English friend, Karen Webster for the lovely photo of her Christening dress. My long-time tea friends, Wendy Chessum and Lydia Hocking, who read and re-read the manuscript. The wonderful friendship and endless pots of tea with Jessica Avery, owner of The House of Commons Tea Room in Denver, and to Helen Benziger, great-granddaughter of Margaret Brown, for her friendship and creative information. And finally to all those wonderful grandchildren who never say "no" to sharing tea with Grams.

·

Table of Contents

Acknowledgments · xiii
Introduction · xvii
Main Characters of Downton Abbey · · · · · · · · · · · · · · · · xxi
Chapter 1   The Real Downton Abbey - Highclere Castle · · · · · · · · · · 1
Chapter 2   The History and Tradition of Tea · · · · · · · · · · · · · · · · 9
Chapter 3   A Life of Service · 19
Chapter 4   High Tea · 27
Chapter 5   The Manners and Etiquette of Tea Time · · · · · · · · · · · · 53
Chapter 6   The Gift of Hospitality · 63
Chapter 7   The Pleasures of Tea · 71
Chapter 8   Downton Abbey Tea · 77
Chapter 9   Celebrating Birthdays · 103
Chapter 10 A Christening Tea · 121
Chapter 11 Children's Tea Party · 141
Chapter 12 English Christmas and Tea · 167
Chapter 13 Molly Brown Comes to Tea · · · · · · · · · · · · · · · · · · · 199
Chapter 14 Tea on the Titanic · 215
Making the Perfect Cup of Tea · 235
Storing Tea · 237
Tea for a Crowd · 239
Sandwich Making Tips · 241
Recipe Index · 243
Illustrations · 247

Introduction

• • •

THE FIRST TIME I WATCHED *Downton Abbey* I was hooked. I wondered if it would it be a repeat of *Upstairs, Downstairs*. Not knowing what to expect, I kept watching, week after week, until I was totally immersed in a period drama. I was not alone. I joined more than 200 million viewers in more than 200 countries around the world. We would be glued to the telly on Sunday nights watching life unfold for a fictional upper-class family and their downstairs servants on PBS Masterpiece Theatre.

I had just completed writing my book, *Tea on the Titanic*, and had been researching that very same period of time of a class-based society in the Edwardian era. First, second, and third-class passengers were all under one roof on the ship, similar, but *Downton Abbey* was set on dry land. The opening scene involves the latest news of the *Titanic* being lost at sea, and an heir from *Downton Abbey* one of its victims. The series follows the lives of the fictitious Crawley family who live in a lovely, old, grand English country home. The series begins in 1912 and will complete season six in the 1920s.

Downton Abbey reminds me of my English heritage. Every trip across the pond is special. I visit my birthplace, very near Oxford, and find a manor house for afternoon tea. I arrive on the graveled drive and approach the front door. I could very well be a character in a Jane Austen book. There is a slight drizzle of rain, and the butler with the oversized green and white striped umbrella rushes out and opens my car door. I am usherd into the Laura Ashley-inspired parlor all set for afternoon tea. A fire is flickering in the fireplace as I sink into the over-stuffed chairs. The silver tea service is placed on the table, tea is poured, and I am experiencing *Downton Abbey*. Was this not my cup of tea!

I have researched the Edwardian era, including the etiquette, manners, social customs, fashions and recipes for my last two books, *Tea on the Titanic* and *First Class Etiquette*. It seemed an opportune time to continue my love of that era with a book relating to tea at *Downton Abbey*.

The actors who portray the cast of *Downton Abbey* are almost all English, including the Producer and Director, Julian Fellows. One must assume that they all have been brought up with tea as a large part of their lives. They represent the three distinct classes (rich, middle, and lower) of the Edwardian period in real life and also the characters they portray. Money and position in society made the difference between living at *Downton Abbey* or working there.

An interesting and unique aspect of *Downton Abbey* is the single voice of the lone writer on the show, Julian Fellows, a master craftsman at creating story and character. He is very real how he deals with everyday life, both upstairs and the sagas of the servants.

The popularity of the show started with nine million viewers representing more than 200 countries. As the series progresses, the numbers keep climbing. The audience finds this time-frame fascinating. It is similar to the movie *Titanic*, with its staggering box office sales of over $2.2 billion worldwide, and revolved around the same Edwardian era.

What keeps everyone so enamored of *Downton Abbey*? There is a lot to like. The characters form a complex group. The story-line is well written, the costumes are fabulous, the country manor house is the real thing, and the actors are some of Britain's best. The show appeals to different audiences in different ways. For Americans, we have always found British manners and the formality of a class system intriguing. Julian Fellows told The New York Times, "I think most of the stories are about emotional situations that everyone can understand." We love to watch the proprieties of the upstairs Crawleys and the diverse personalities of the staff. It appeals to such a vast range of the population, all ages, male and female.

Since writing my book, *Tea on the Titanic*, and speaking to groups of women all over the United States, I found they love to recreate the grandeur of the Edwardian era and specifically a *Titanic* Tea. Therefore, with the amazing interest in *Downton Abbey*, my desire is to share with you how to recreate your own *Downton Abbey* tea.

Main Characters of Downton Abbey

• • •

The Crawley Family

Violet Crawley
(Dowager Countess of Grantham and Robert and Rosamund's Mother)

Robert Crawley (Lord Grantham or Earl of Grantham)

Cora Crawley (nee Levinson, Countess of Grantham - Robert's wife)

Lady Rosamund Painswick (nee Crawley - Robert's sister)

Lady Mary Crawley, Lady Edith Crawley, Lady Sybil Crawley
(Daughters of Robert and Cora Crawley)

Extended Family

Isobel Crawley
(Mother of Matthew Crawley)

Matthew Crawley (Lord Grantham's third cousin)
(Husband of Lady Mary)

Tom Branson
(Former family chauffeur and husband of Lady Sybil)

The Downstairs Staff

Mr. Charles Carson   Mrs. Elsie Hughes
(Head Butler)   (Housekeeper)

Mr. John Bates   Mrs. Beryl Patmore
(Lord Grantham's Valet)   (Head Cook)

Thomas Barrow (Under Butler)   Anna Smith (Lady Mary's Maid)

Daisy Robinson (Kitchen Maid)

High Clere Castle Photo by Carol Spurway

CHAPTER 1

The Real Downton Abbey - Highclere Castle

• • •

HIGHCLERE CASTLE, A REAL PLACE in the countryside of England, is the setting for the award-winning series, *Downton Abbey*, on PBS Masterpiece Theater. The personal home to the 8th Earl and Countess of Carnarvon, Highclere Castle has been the family home for more than three hundred years. Originally built as an estate for the Bishops of Winchester (the reason it is called an abbey) more than 800 years ago, the castle currently serves as a popular place for visitors from all over the world. The majority are fans of *Downton Abbey*. The Castle sits on five thousand acres of lush gardens and rolling hills, five times larger than Central Park in New York City.

Lord Carnarvon, the 8th Earl of Carnarvon, is the current owner of the castle and lives with his wife, Lady Fiona. Queen Elizabeth is the Earl's godmother. He is very interested in all areas of farming and its role in England. Highclere Castle utilizes more than two thousand acres of rich farmland to grow crops for horse and human consumption. The horse feed, mainly oats, grown and packaged at the castle, provides the favored brand for Queen Elizabeth's horses. This operation helps the Carnarvons raise revenue for the high costs of upkeep and restoration of the castle.

Before chosen as the set for the television series, Highclere Castle was in desperate need of repairs. It was estimated that the restoration and repairs would cost almost twelve million pounds (nineteen million dollars) for the extensive water damage, crumbling stone, and collapsed ceilings. Because of the popularity of the series, the Carnarvon family has been able to do all the repairs and restore the house to its former glory. Highclere is open to the public for several months each year, which also brings in revenue.

Approaching Highclere Castle on the mile-long, gravel drive, the main tower of the castle is what is first seen as it emerges from the often present fog. At this point, the haunting theme song from *Downton Abbey* becomes close to audible. The Scottish-born, Emmy award-winning composer, John Lunn, utilizes a 35-piece string orchestra, a solo piano, and a French horn. The music marries one scene to the next. It's a simple melody that seemingly goes along with the dialog. Once you hear it, you won't forget the familiar strain.

Julian Fellows, the Oscar-winning screenwriter for *Downton Abbey*, chose Highclere Castle as he believed it would be the perfect setting for his series. Highclere Castle is located in North Hampshire, about 70 miles west of London, near the town of Newbury, (pronounced "Newbree.") The prestigious racetrack, The Racecourse Newbury, draws thousands of spectators to its thoroughbred races. The Queen of England frequently attends the racecourse to watch her horses race. An international antique and collectors fair, also at Racecourse Newbury, draws thousands of spectators and trade buyers from around the globe. Newbury profits from the international attention that *Downton Abbey* has brought to this ordinary town. This new found attention thrills the cabbies with the increased demand to drive passengers to the castle from the train station, as well as the shops selling Highclere souvenirs, which are now highly demanded by tourists.

The castle underwent modernization many times in the past two centuries. The current owners enjoy living in the castle and involve themselves in the daily castle activities, especially in the production of

Downton Abbey. The architect, Sir Charles Berry, (1795 -1860) designer of the Palace of Westminster, known to most of us as Big Ben, had no idea his work would be enjoyed to this day by millions of viewers around the world. At one time, Highclere Castle employed as many as 60 full-time servants to run the extensive estate. After World War 1 and the massive destruction of England from the bombing, taxes skyrocketed from six-percent to more than 60 percent. Many of the owners of the large manor houses lost the ability to have servants or simply keep their properties. They became land rich, but cash poor. Thus, began the change of the landscape throughout England, and, sadly, more than 1,200 stately homes were demolished for lack of maintenance funds. The innovations of finding creative ways to finance manors emerged from many people, including the Carnarvons. Farming, house tours, weddings, corporate events, and location sites for filming, keeps Highclere, and many other grand homes, standing today.

Perfect landscapes permeate the gardens at Highclere. They still hold true to the original garden's blueprint of the famous landscape designer of the 1700's, Lancelot "Capability" Brown. He earned his title by declaring a country estate could have a great "capability" for improvement. His work continues to be admired in the gardens of Highclere Castle. Capability Brown's garden designs reside throughout England. A particularly beautiful magnum opus of his exhibits is at Blemheim Palace, the birthplace of Winston Churchill.

Highclere Castle fostered great political activity during the nineteenth and twentieth centuries. Highclere hosted many diplomats, celebrities, aviators, Egyptologists, and royalty for social events. The 5th Earl of Carnarvon and Howard Carter, an English archaeologist, discovered the Egyptian tomb of King Tutankhamun (King Tut) in the early 1920's and brought world awareness to the discovery. Now, part of the tour in the cellar of the Castle displays an Egyptian exhibit.

During World War I, the castle was converted into a hospital by Lady Almina, the 5th Countess of Carnarvon, who led the staff of 30 nurses to care for the wounded soldiers. She became very skilled as a nurse and welcomed the injured into her home. *Downton Abbey* vividly portrays the action of war in amazing detail, as Matthew Crawley, heir to *Downton Abbey*, Thomas Barrow, footman/valet, and William Mason, also a footman, go off to war during Season Two. Many of the staff and the Crawley family are actively engaged in caring for the injured. From the real Highclere Castle, more than 75 men, mainly the groomsmen and gardeners, went off to war. Thirteen of those men never returned home. One of the bedrooms functioned as an operating room where the war-injured were treated by surgeons from London who volunteered their services each Monday. That room has converted back to the original guest bedroom, the Arundel Bedroom.

Many of the soldiers treated at Highclere Castle during World War I, wrote letters of gratitude to Lady Almina, complimenting her astoundingly gracious hospitality. The soldiers also explained they were treated with the utmost respect. The letters include thanks for lavish dinners, served on the castle's china and crystal, while they were recuperating from their injuries.

The castle also became home to many children during World War II after evacuating from London amidst the blitz bombing. Estimation speculates that nearly two million children were evacuated from London to the countryside of England. Disabled men and women, pregnant women, the elderly, and those who had already lost their homes to the heavy bombing in London were also evacuees. Highclere Castle took in some children, but no records indicate the duration of their stay. The children remained out of the city during the worst of the bombings, and returned home as quickly as possible. Many other stately homes refuged children during that time.

In *Downton Abbey*, some scenes were filmed outside of Highclere Castle, such as the kitchen and village scenes. However, many actual castle locations appear in the show. We can recognize certain rooms while viewing *Downton Abbey*. The red velvet sofas and walls of books of the beautiful library appear often in the show. This room stays close to its true decorum with the nearly 6,000 books on the shelves. In its true existence, this room served as the Drawing Room for most of the 19th century. The furniture, artwork, and accessories are combinations of the intermingling of families and cultures who have lived in the castle.

The Drawing Room of a fine English home equates the American Living Room, the main public room, where guests are entertained. The decor is warm, welcoming, and comfortable, but it is not an informal room. In other words, the Drawing Room is not a place to lie around on the couches to watch television. The term "Drawing Room" came into fashion as the place women would retire after dinner, a smaller private room attatched to a more public room, such as the Dining Room – to withdraw, so the men could stay in the Dining Room to share their cigars and port.

On a recent visit to England, I visited No. 1 Royal Crescent in Bath, the flagship museum of the Bath Preservation Trust. My cousin John and I listened to a guide tell the history of the Drawing Room or Parlor. John asked if this room might also have been called the "Lounge." The guide let us know in very precise terms that Lounge was rather a "common or nasty" word for Parlor. We were quickly informed that Lounge is used for a middle-class English home, while Parlor and Drawing Room are distinctly reserved for the upper class! We both had a good laugh and were reminded of our place in society!

Other scenes for *Downtown Abbey* are filmed in a studio in Ealing, a suburb of London. Highclere Castle modernized its kitchen like most of the interior of the castle and lost the original charisma suited for filming a period piece. Owners of most Victorian-era buildings remodel basement interiors, leaving no choice but to recreate the kitchen and servants quarters on a studio set.

Bampton is a village 40 miles north of Highclere Castle that served as the set for filming the fictional village of Downton. With a population of 2,500, the village is small and quaint. However, tourist numbers recently soared and many hoped to spot a star from the series.

Built to impress, Highclere Castle still ranks high among those who require a unique venue for weddings, engagement parties, receptions, private parties, and corporate events. The knowledgeable staff of the castle accommodate the most discerning client. Three of the most popular actors in England are the stars of *Downton Abbey*: Maggie Smith, Hugh Bonneville, and Penelope Wilton. Their star power strongly pulls a large audience to visit and utilize the venue. The price tag for renting the castle for a one-day wedding runs around $30,000. However, walking down the sweeping staircase in your wedding gown might just be worth the high price. Whether there is a wedding or not during your next trip to England, the majestic Highclere Castle is not a place to miss!

CHAPTER 2

The History and Tradition of Tea

• • •

"Wouldn't it be dreadful to live in a country where they didn't have tea?"

Noel Coward

TEA IS AN INTERESTING AND broad word, as it has many meanings and uses. Some of us may think of it as a beverage that has been around for thousands of years, or it may mean a botanical mixture made with hot water, or it can refer to the lovely ceremony of sharing a pot of tea and dainty sandwiches and cakes with friends. This chapter will refer to both the drink and the ceremony.

The pleasure of drinking tea dates back more than 5,000 years. There are two interesting legends regarding the discovery of tea. One tells the story of a Chinese Emperor named Shen Nung, who was sitting under a tree boiling water for purification. A gust of wind blew leaves into his kettle and greatly improved the taste of the water. The Emperor enjoyed his first cup of tea. The second legend gives the discovery to a Buddhist monk from India. He was traveling in China to begin nine years of meditation. During his fifth year, he suffered a time of great fatigue and found it impossible to continue. He chewed some twigs and leaves from a nearby tree and at once was restored. That tree happened to be a tea tree. Whatever the truth behind either of these legends, tea has become a favored part of peoples' lives, and every aspect of the flavorful leaves is interesting.

Whether you might be enjoying the glorious sunshine and a delightful cup of tea on the lush manicured lawn at *Downton Abbey*, or imagine yourself sipping tea in the library of the Titanic, the history of tea provides a glimpse into the past of a great British tradition. While the clothing styles have changed since the Edwardian era, not too much else has changed in the way we enjoy tea. It's the same plant that gives us the leaves that revive and invigorate. Tea appeals to all social classes, from the worker in the shops, who can only stop to have a quick cup of tea, to the "Lady of the House," who enjoys the ceremony of afternoon tea with all the customs followed "to a tea."

The leaves that revitalize and restore health are from the Camellia Senesis bush, a member of the evergreen family that thrives best in fertile, hilly regions. Tea bushes are grown on plantations or estates in approximately forty countries. India is by far the world's largest producer and exporter of tea. The plant, with its shiny green leaves, takes about five years to develop, but then can be harvested several times a month. Only the tip and the top two leaves of the youngest shoots are picked. These freshly picked leaves are spread out on trays in shaded sheds, allowing moisture to evaporate from the leaves. The leaves are then exposed to heat and go through a process of fermentation or oxidation, producing changes in color and fragrance. The leaves are sorted through a series of screens, beginning with large openings and continuing to a very fine mesh. The larger tea leaves usually produce the better grade of tea. The smallest leaves are called "dust" or "fannings" and are used in tea bags.

There are four main types of tea, all coming from the same plant, the Camellia Sinesis:

1. White Tea - very little processing, picked once a year, light sweet taste.

2. Green Tea - unfermented (not exposed to heat), delicate taste and light green color.
3. Oolong Tea - semi-fermented, cross between black and green tea in color and taste.
4. Black Tea - fully fermented, yields a hearty flavor and darker brew and is the most popular tea.

Tea is very economical, yielding 300 cups of tea per pound, and is second to water as the most consumed beverage in the world. It is one of the few drinks that has no sodium, no fat, no carbohydrates, no sugar, and no calories. Tea must contain leaves from the Camellia Senesis plant in order to be called "tea." Herbal "teas" are products of fruits, flowers, leaves, bark, seeds, or roots from plants other than the tea plant. These drinks are "tisanes" or "infusions," and are usually caffeine-free. All tea from the Camellia Senesis bush, including green tea, has caffeine.

While tea had great popularity in the Orient, it did not arrive in Europe until the mid-1600s and was first served at a coffee house in London. In England, it quickly replaced the national drink of ale. Tea mania had arrived!

A traditional afternoon tea ceremony dates back 160 years to Victorian England, then continued into the Edwardian era, and is still popular today. We can thank Anna, the 7th Duchess of Bedford and Queen Victoria's lady in waiting, who popularized the delightful art of afternoon tea in the mid-1800s. Since dinner was served late, Anna began to have "a sinking feeling" (hypoglycemia?) and felt rather peckish mid-afternoon. She asked her servants to bring a tray with tea and cookies to her sitting room. The nourishment gave her a much needed energy boost and kept her energized until the dinner hour. This little snack quickly became a popular pastime within her circle of friends, and the tradition of afternoon tea spread throughout the British aristocracy.

At that time, the newly created middle class began to adopt the ritual as well. Without the luxurious homes with sitting rooms and conservatories, they began to go out to tea shops. The first tea shops were opened in London by the Aerated Bread Company in the mid 1800's as ABC Tea Shops. Then the Lyons Tea Company began to compete and London was a mecca for tea lovers.

Queen Victoria continued this ritual, hosting lavish afternoon tea parties in the garden of Buckingham Palace. The reason many afternoon teas today are called "Victorian Teas" is from this association with Queen Victoria. Today, Queen Elizabeth II keeps this tradition alive by holding three afternoon teas in the Rose Garden of Buckingham Palace every summer, and one at Holyrood House in Edinburgh. The invited guests, more than 8,000 per event, are subjects who have served England well in numerous capacities.

They start arriving at the palace around 3 p.m. and mingle in the garden, drinking more than 27,000 cups of tea. Every year about 32,000 Britons receive hand-written invitations from the Lord Chamberlain's office at Buckingham Palace to attend the garden tea. It is impossible to request admission to one of the parties, as one must be appointed by a royal approved sponsor. The Queen and her husband the Duke of Edinburgh, with other members of the Royal Family, arrive at 4 p.m. and circulate among the guests for several hours.

Several years ago, British friends of ours were invited to one of the Garden Party Teas at Buckingham Palace. Lyn and her husband Alan both worked for the United Kingdom Atomic Energy Authority when they were notified they had been selected to represent their company at the tea. The invitation from the Queen arrived at their home several months before the event. Lyn told me, "Never in my wildest dreams did I ever think I would be having tea with the Queen at Buckingham Palace! I grew up in a working class family and lived in Council housing (government assistance), so what chance did I have for such an adventure?" But off they went to London to have tea with the Queen; Alan dressed in his suit and tie, and Lyn in her best dress with a fascinator on her head.

In the garden, the guests were served tea in china tea cups and saucers, and dined on dainty tea sandwiches and pastries. The Queen and the Duke of Edinburgh arrived about 4 p.m. and circulated among the guests.

Those people who actually met the Queen had been selected before the event, and were dignitaries and ambassadors. Everyone was able to walk freely around the 42 acres of the palace garden, visit with the other guests, and perhaps have the opportunity to chat with other members of the Royal Family. Lyn and Alan mingled with Prince Charles, Prince Andrew, Prince Edward, and Princess Anne. This was a day that will always be a very special part of their lives. I only wish I could have been there, too!

In Victorian and Edwardian times tea was very expensive, and usually kept in a tea caddy, a locked wooden or tin box that held two or three types of tea. A tea caddy was of great importance in the household, as tea blending was usually done in each home instead of commercially prepared as it is done today. Most of the tea caddies had three containers inside: one for black tea, one for green tea, and the third for blending the two teas. The lady of the house kept a key to the caddy on a chain or ribbon around her neck to keep the servants from using the "good" tea. As tea became more popular and affordable, the use of a tea caddy diminished, and today is more of a collectible item than a necessity. At *Downton Abbey*, I am sure Mrs. Hughes, the housekeeper, kept control of the tea caddy key at all times.

It is hard to believe that barely a hundred years ago, tea was only for the wealthy or royalty in Western societies. Today, it is a daily beverage of millions. Instead of keeping the classes separated by having tea in private dining quarters, teatime is a great way to bring friends together and to grow relationships.

As quoted in National Geographic, reporter Dan Stone states, "The world's most consumed beverage – not counting water, which has no equal – is actually a dark horse, the kind you don't suspect. It's not coffee, nor Coca Cola, and it's surprisingly not even beer. It's tea." Over six billion cups of tea are consumed daily worldwide. We are in good company – us tea drinkers. As wonderful as it is would be to have tea in a lovely old manor house such as Highclere Castle, nothing is more pleasant than having friends for tea in your home.

My great-grandparents lived in the northeast of England, and owned a business providing household help to wealthy families near Sandringham, the country retreat of the royal family. Queen Mary, the grandmother of

Queen Elizabeth II, called at their home to discuss the employment of several housemaids. My great-grandmother quickly brought the tea trolley into the parlor and made the Queen a cup of tea. A wooden tea caddy on the trolley contained her special blend of tea. Several years ago, I received that very tea caddy from a family member, who knew I would be thrilled to own such a royal treasure.

As a child on one of our family trips to England, we went to Sandringham to tour the grounds. We were given a "heads up" that Queen Mary would be back in several hours to inspect the carpentry shop we were visiting. We rushed back to our hotel and quickly changed clothes, practiced our curtsies and bows, and were instructed not to speak to the Queen unless we were spoken to first. We had the great honor of meeting Queen Mary and visiting with her for about 15 minutes. She did most of the talking and was very interested in America. Among the things she discussed was her son, the former King Edward VIII, who had abdicated the throne and married an American, Wallis Simpson. The Queen wanted to know where we lived in America and was it close to New York City. She also asked my Mother where she was from in England and did she know Sandringham. She also inquired to our length of stay in England. My mother, a staunch royalist, was overjoyed to have this visit with the Queen and actually asked the Queen to pose for a picture, which she did. Had I known the story of the tea caddy at that time, I would have asked Queen Mary if she remembered my great-grandmother. This was one of my most cherished memories of our trip and I continue to tell this wonderful story.

Teas at *Downton Abbey* and on the *Titanic* would have been very similar to the teas given by Queen Victoria and Queen Mary. The table would have been an impressive sight with the fine bone china, linen napkins, silver teaspoons, and the food served on silver tiers. Flavored teas were not popular at that time, so a black tea, Darjeeling or Earl Grey, would have been the choices. Because large county homes and ocean liners at that time held dining and service as high priorities, nothing would have been left to chance. Mrs. Patmore, the cook at *Downton Abbey*, and the Head Chef, Charles Proctor, on the *Titanic*, would have carefully planned the afternoon tea. Dainty tea sandwiches, freshly baked scones, served with the traditional clotted cream and jam, fresh fruit tartlets, and crisp buttery shortbread, would have been meticulously arranged.

In today's tea world, tea companies employ tea-blenders, each with their own recipes for a variety of teas. The International Tea Masters Association provides certification to those individuals who desire to become specialists. A certified tea blender learns all aspects of tea preparation, the history of each tea, and how to do tea tastings. The skill of the tea blender ensures the taste of the tea will be the same with each batch. Some of the blends might contain as many as 30 different teas. An English breakfast tea from one company might taste very different than another of the same name, because of the recipe used by the tea-blender.

I had never thought of blending my own teas until I had a conglomeration of tea tins, each with small amounts of tea. I combined the teas and had some interesting blends. It is a great way to use up small amounts of tea. About that same time I had an opportunity to meet "Fergie", Sarah, the Duchess of York, who was in Los Angeles promoting her new book, *Dining with the Duchess*. She was charming and very friendly, so I took the opportunity to ask her what was her favorite tea. She said, "Oh, I love to mix my teas, let me write it down for you." So, she took my book and on page 189, she wrote, "Lapsang Souchang and Earl Grey mixed." She told me to mix equal parts of each tea. She then inscribed, "To Penelope, Sarah the Duchess of York." Ever since that meeting, I love to mix teas, but my favorite is now Earl Grey and Lapsang Souchang!

Earl Grey is probably the most popular tea blend and its title conjures an image of something quite royal. It is named after the 2nd Earl Grey, who was Prime Minister of England from 1830 to 1834. The legend credits a Mandarin Chinese man who gave the tea or a recipe for the tea to the Earl as a gift for saving his son's life. Twinings Tea and Jacksons of Piccadilly Tea both claim that they have the original Earl Grey tea recipe! A traditional Earl Grey blend will have a medium strength of black tea flavored with the oil of Bergamot (a small pear-shaped fruit grown in Italy, similar to an orange, but with a very distinctive taste). The flavor of each tea varies according to the producer and the recipe, as well as the area of the leaves' growth, as also with wine.

Flavored teas were not sold commercially until about 1945. Now every tea company has hundreds of varieties. Many are flavored with oils, real fruits, leaves, or flowers, all providing an abundance of choices. There are teas for every kind of social occasion; from a child's tea to the tea served in the boardroom for businessmen. But it all goes back to taking time to sit down with others and have a cup of tea.

During the Edwardian era, tea was only available as loose tea. In 1908, Thomas Sullivan, a tea importer in New York, began to send out his tea samples in little silk pouches instead of tins to reduce his cost. He soon began to get increased orders, but he was rather confused when the customers complained that the tea was not arriving in the little bags, but still in the loose-leaf form. Slowly the tea industry began the business of selling tea in tea bags. Today, the majority of tea sold worldwide is tea bags. As popular as tea bags are, tea made with loose-leaf tea is superior in taste. I might be challenged on this point, but the proof is in the "pudding"! If you are a coffee drinker, I shall use the analogy of instant coffee or fresh brewed coffee. Or fresh peas and canned peas? There is a big difference.

Iced tea is very common in our culture and accounts for 80 to 85 percent of tea consumed in America. It usually is a summer-time drink for most of us, and is even served at afternoon teas. It became popular during the 1904 World's Fair in St. Louis. The weather was very warm and humid, and hot tea wasn't selling well. A tea merchant borrowed some ice from the neighboring ice cream vendor and soon had a long line of customers for his cool drink. In the southern states, tea has been poured over ice for many years. Many old cookbooks, from as early as the 1880s, have recipes for tea punches that combined tea with wines, champagnes, and liquors, all served over ice.

One summer, our English cousins came to visit us in Southern California. We were at a restaurant for dinner and everyone ordered tea.

When the server brought everyone a tall glass of iced tea, my cousins looked confused. We explained the need to mention "hot" when placing a tea order. Just the opposite is true in England, as it is always served hot. The server will ask, "black or white?" Black has no milk; white is served with milk.

Tea is not just a tradition in England; it is a way of life. I hope you will be able to envision how the traditions of tea have traveled far and wide, beginning with those of wealth and position, and then passed down to the average person. Tea was for everyone at *Downton Abbey*, upstairs and downstairs, and also on the *Titanic*, all three classes of passengers; but the elegant settings and careful preparations are what still "invite" our attention.

> *"You can never get a cup of tea large enough*
> *or a book long enough to suit me."*

-C.S. Lewis

CHAPTER 3

A Life of Service

• • •

Downstairs at *Downton Abbey*

THE UPSTAIRS LIFE AT *DOWNTON Abbey* ran smoothly because of the down-stairs staff. The passengers on the *Titanic*, all three classes, had a "holiday" trip because of all the crew on board. Every stately home, manor house, or ocean liner in the early 20th century had staffs to cover all the tasks that were necessary to keep a home with 50 rooms running well, or an ocean-going vessel "ship-shape." It is astounding to think of the costs to pay for the 60 staff members to run *Downton Abbey* and the grounds, or the 900 crew members on the *Titanic*.

The culture of that era ran on a class system, and even the service help operated by a hierarchy. At the top of the social order was the butler, then the housekeeper, the lady's maids, the valets, the footmen, the cooks, and the chauffeurs; plus all the assistants and the various positions on the out-side. To sneak a peek into the lives of those in service at *Downton Abbey*, we only get a little glimmer of how hard and long the days were for most of them. Up before dawn and to bed very late, was the life of a house servant. While viewing the servant's plight in *Downton Abbey* as being rather pleas-ant, with decent and clean bedrooms and baths, the majority of servants in the late 19ᵗʰ century lived a meager existence. The fact that they had jobs at *Downton Abbey*, working for an Earl, was a good thing...it meant they excelled at their jobs and had the benefit of job security. On the *Titanic*, a hierarchy also existed for the staff, from the Captain down through the ranks of postal workers, orchestra members, waiters, maids, attendants, firemen, cooks, and cleaners.

My friend George was a butler for many years in Europe in his younger days. He is the only butler I have ever known, and I thought it would be interesting to get his input into the current interest in service staffs from an expert. George fell into his job when he was bar-tending in Switzerland. One of his regular customers was a governess for a local family who were about to lose their butler. The husband and wife both went to the bar and had a few drinks as they interviewed George. I asked George if he had any experience before this job as a butler. "No," he said, "but I had been a head-waiter in banquet service at a Radisson Hotel in North Carolina." After he was hired, he knew the referral meant more than his experience. His job as a butler was serving meals; breakfast, lunch and dinner. He worked a split shift from 8 a.m. to 2 p.m., with free time until he returned to the house at 5 p.m. and worked until midnight or later. In Europe, all service staff are provided with housing, meals, medical benefits, and social security. He did not live with the family, but had his own apartment.

His relationship with his employer was always on a professional basis with no personal involvement with the family of four. George continues to have a professional respect for the family he served more than 30 years ago. He was careful not to divulge any personal information. I gathered that George's employers were very wealthy, as there was a staff of five and only four family members! Loyalty to the employer is one of the key components in each of the staff at *Downton Abbey*. Because the staff is always in the background and within earshot of the family discussing private concerns, loyalty is essential. By contrast, the upstairs family would know very little of the servants lives. When I asked George if he would consider being a butler again, he responded quickly with a "yes, but only if I were younger."

Probably not many of us have had the privilege of having a full-time housekeeper, cook, or butler. During certain times in my life, I have had a cleaning lady and felt it was part of my sanity plan. My grandparents in England always had a housekeeper and cook, so when my mother came to America as a young bride, she was not well prepared for the cooking and upkeep of a home. Her cooking was by trial and fire – literally, as many of our meals were over cooked. But by the time I was old enough to help in the kitchen, she had become proficient enough to teach me. Her love of hospitality overshadowed the lack of expertise in the kitchen.

We all loved the story of my mother baking bread. She thought it would be nice if our family could enjoy freshly baked bread and proceeded to prepare the dough. When it had risen and was ready to bake, she asked my father how long it should stay in the oven. He thought about 5 hours! Needless to say, that loaf of bread would have stayed intact if she had pitched it all the way across the ocean, home to England.

In the early part of the 20th century there was much excitement to be chosen for a job in a big house as a servant. There was not much choice for a career as a woman in those days, but being a maid, a lady's maid, or housekeeper would have given a girl the chance for employment and an advantage to improve her marriage prospects. Young ladies waited with anticipation when the owner of a big house brought his housekeeper to their school to choose new maids from the classroom. While the hours would be long and strenuous, the girls were able to release their families from the financial burdens of housing, clothing, and food, as the employers would provide those basic necessities. Since servants were housed and fed by their masters, having a job in service was much more desirable than working in factories and farms, and there was always the chance for promotion.

The upstairs life was so dependent on the downstairs staff, it would be unfair to say that life was not tolerable, because once the work for the day was over, the staff had time for themselves. They might play games, read, gossip or catch up on the events of the day. In *Downton Abbey*, we see the best accommodations and lifestyles that those in service could have. Mrs. Patmore, the cook, provided the menus for both the family upstairs, and for the whole staff of at least 50. In reality, she would have had more than one assistant in order to keep the kitchen open and running for both upstairs and downstairs.

Because of the large number of employees both at *Downton Abbey* and on the *Titanic*, there were rules for the servants to obey. Many came from homes that lacked the most basic social graces, so it was important that they knew what was expected of them. They were to keep their opinions to themselves, keep their voices low and soft, never begin a conversation with the members of the family, not speak to another servant if a family member was present, and not fraternize with the opposite sex. If items were broken in the house, the amount to replace the damaged goods would be deducted from their wages. This seemed rather severe for those who gave so much, were paid so little, but were still expected to "know their place."

> *"There are rules to this way of life… and if you're not prepared*
> *to live by them, then it's not the right life for you."*

- Mrs. Hughes

On board the *Titanic*, the crew and staff worked from dawn to dusk and beyond. Many of the passengers had their personal servants with them, so there was an over-lapping of duties for those who worked in First-Class. The accommodations for many of the First-Class passengers were suites that included a room for the personal servants. Staff were served their meals in their rooms or in the dining area on C deck with the crew.

I wonder if they compared assignments. While cooking for a staff of 50 seems daunting enough, imagine the planning and bringing that amount of food on board for more than 2500! We can only speculate who ate "where" and "what," as there are no menus or recorded data about where the staff ate. It is likely that they enjoyed food prepared in the First and Second class kitchens. We know Captain Smith was the guest at several of the personal dining events for the First-Class passengers, but the majority of the staff dined together.

While upstairs, the Crawleys at *Downton Abbey* dined on fine china and crystal, with linen tablecloths and napkins. Dining was very important in the lives of the upper class in Edwardian England. It was a significant time for the Crawley family while eating a meal. The staff was highly skilled at presenting advanced and elaborate cuisines. Even though the servants ate at the long wooden table downstairs in the servants' dining hall, the tables were set with cloth napkins and food was served in a very civilized style.

Before World War I, there was an abundance of working-class Brits who served as domestic servants both in middle-class and upper-class homes. After the war, many of the domestic help never returned from the trenches, and with the diminished supply of servants, there was not the manpower to produce time-consuming menus. The quality of life of those living upstairs, depended on the downstairs staff. Plus, the shipments of produce and other food sources were rationed. However, *Downton Abbey* and most stately homes of that time had food grown on the estate. Not only did the Crawleys eat well, but also the staff, as everyone benefited from organic farming.

Most of the food we see served during the filming on the set of *Downton Abbey* was not edible. It was prepared in advance by food stylist, Lisa Heathcote. The complexity of preparing food and keeping it looking fresh after eight hours under bright lights, with no refrigeration, presented a huge challenge. In reality, menus at a manor house would have been planned by the cook, approved by the housekeeper, with the final consent coming from the Lady of the house.

Each season gives us a glorious rendition of how those upstairs dined. It was a formal meal with starters (hors d'oeuvres), soup, a fish dish, entrees (beef and foul), vegetables, dessert, cheese, fruit and crackers or nuts, followed by coffee and cigars for the men, with brandy or port – a very big deal. Downstairs, the staff did not eat until the family had finished their meal. It might be some of the same food that was served upstairs, a savory, vegetables, bread, and probably a pudding (dessert). This is "high tea," the evening meal or supper of the working class, not to be confused with the more elaborate "afternoon tea" that would be served the upper class before dinner, later in the afternoon. Of course, there was always the proverbial pot of tea. The staff on the *Titanic* had their evening meal very similar to the Third-Class passengers. The preparations for the lavish meals for the First and Second-classes were completed before the staff could have their evening meal. It didn't matter whether on land or sea, "high tea" was served to those in service.

CHAPTER 4

High Tea

• • •

"The tea of the English working-class is the most eccentric of meals,
and one of the greatest injuries a gourmet could possibly conceive…
it must shock anyone endowed with refined epicurean instinct."

J. REY IN *THE WHOLE ART OF DINING,* 1914

WE HAVE ALL BEEN TO tearooms that advertise "high" tea, and quickly realize it is the same as the last "afternoon" tea we attended in another tearoom. Why does one establishment call it "high" tea and another "afternoon" tea? Can we expect to be watching an episode of *Downton Abbey* where the staff is serving "high tea" in the drawing room of the castle, while the servants downstairs are also having "high tea" in the kitchen?

High Tea is the evening meal or supper served downstairs at *Downton Abbey* in the Servants Hall to the staff, and the meal served the crew on the *Titanic.* The working classes arrived home very tired and hungry after a long day in the factories or shops. The evening meal would involve a mug of tea, bread, vegetables (sometimes meat) and cheese. It was not a social event or the gap between lunch and dinner, but a necessity. Today, high tea is served all seasons of the year. It's usually quick and simple, and prepared with a minimum of advance planning. The meal can include one or more savory items, followed by a dessert, or "pud" as the English call it. The choices for tea are numerous and can include fruit teas, herbal teas, or a decaffeinated tea. Usually served after 5 p.m., this delightful tea can be a prelude to an evening of games, a movie, or a play.

High tea takes the place of dinner and is served at a regular or normal dining table, hence "high tea", not like afternoon tea that can be enjoyed while seated in low comfortable chairs around a coffee table. It is usually served in the kitchen and not as formal as an afternoon tea. Table settings should include a tablecloth or placemats, cloth napkins, teacups and saucers, or tea mugs. High tea is not a step-down dining option, just a more relaxed and casual affair. The "high" in afternoon teas served at tearooms and hotels, usually refers to the price, not the style of tea service. It has become more popular for some hotels in England to advertise their afternoon tea service as a "high tea in London" as so many of their customers are from foreign countries that refer to afternoon tea as high tea.

Several years ago I planned a tea for a bridal shower. Since the guests could not attend an afternoon tea, a high tea was planned for the evening. I had reservations about not having a proper "Afternoon Tea," as one of the guests was the wife of a social emissary. This couple traveled extensively in Europe and even dined with royals and dignitaries. I wanted everything to be perfect. I needlessly worried, as she told me later that it was one of the most "glorious" teas she had ever attended!

The menu for high tea will not include little dainty sandwiches, but more substantial and traditional English hot dishes. In addition to a savory course, scones, and pudding (dessert), you may include a fruit or green salad. The scones or bread are always served with the savory course during a high tea and not with clotted cream. If you are a connoisseur of lovely English afternoon teas, you might agree with the opening statement of this chapter. However, I hope you will give an authentic "high" tea a chance to win you over!

Menu for High Tea
Choose 1 or 2 from each category

Savory Course

Beans on Toast
Cornish Pasty
Sausage Rolls
Scotch Eggs
Scottish Stovies
Toad in the Hole
Cottage Pie

Scones

Irish Potato Scones
Cheese Scones
Honey Scones
Beer or Ale Bread
Irish Soda Bread
Crumpets

Desserts

English Trifle
Lemon Coconut Poppy Seed Cake
Rachel's Sticky Toffee Pudding
British Bread and Butter Pudding
Sauce for Bread and Butter Pudding

Teas

English Black Tea
Earl Grey
Mango Decaffeinated

Savory Course

Choose one or more of the following savory recipes for the first-course. A fresh-fruit salad or tossed green salad is a nice addition to these dishes.

Beans on Toast

When I was growing up, we had this many Sunday evenings. Almost every Sunday for lunch we had Roast Beef and potatoes, with roasted vegetables. My Mum liked to do something quick and easy for tea.

Toast
1 can of Heinz beans or baked beans

It can't get much easier than this. I usually don't use Heinz beans as they are rather bland. American Baked Beans have brown sugar and maybe a little barbecue sauce…but growing up it was pretty basic. My husband and I add crisp fried bacon pieces and some sharp cheddar cheese on top. Great quick meal!! A real Brit comfort food.

Cornish Pasty (Pastie)

Cornwall is a rocky peninsula that juts out some 90 miles into the Atlantic Ocean. It is a beautiful part of England which offers a dramatic coastline with spectacular beaches, beautiful gardens, and quaint little villages. Cornwall was once home to many tin mines. The pastie was popular with the miners who could eat the meal in the mine without cutlery, and because of its shape, they could hold onto it by the crust, eat it with dirty hands, then throw away the crust. Because of its thick pastry shell, it would stay warm for several hours. There are many variations to a pastie, but the one that is near and dear to my heart is my mother's recipe. As children, we would take these to school in our lunch boxes.

*Piecrust for six– 6-inch rounds

½ pound ground beef
1 small onion, chopped
1 small turnip, chopped
1 medium carrot, cut into small pieces
1 small potato cut into small cubes
Salt and pepper to taste
¼ teaspoon thyme
1 egg, beaten with 1 teaspoon water.

Preheat oven to 350° F
Line a baking sheet with parchment paper

Mix all the ingredients together, except the egg. Spoon 1/6 of the filling into the middle of each pastry round. Spread the filling on the pastry to cover the middle portion, then brush the beaten egg mixture around the pastry edges. Put the edges of the pastry round together to form a half-circle, and press the edges together tightly. Turn the edges slightly, then crimp them with the tines of a fork. Make sure the edges are sealed, to keep the juices in the crust. Brush the pastie with the egg wash. Make several slits on top of each pastie.

Bake on baking sheet about 1 hour, 15 minutes. These are delicious served with ketchup the American style, but my mother thought they were perfect without. Pasties can be baked and then frozen for later use. To reheat, place frozen pastie on a cookie sheet and bake for 20 minutes at 300°F.

*Sue's Pie Crust

    2 cups all-purpose flour
    2/3 cup shortening
    1 Tablespoon sugar
    1 egg
    4 Tablespoons cold water

Measure dry ingredients into large bowl. Cut the shortening into the flour mixture with a pastry blender or cutter.

Blend until the dough looks like coarse corn meal. In a smaller bowl, mix the egg and the cold water. Pour the egg mixture into the flour mixture and blend until all of flour mixture is absorbed. Divide the dough into six balls and roll out each ball onto a floured surface into a 6-inch round.

My friend Sue Hart gave me this recipe many years ago. She says it is as close to a no-fail recipe as you can get! Her aunt gave her this recipe many years ago, which came from a church cookbook printed in the early 1900s.

Sausage Rolls

The frozen puff pastry would have saved Mrs. Patmore and Daisy hours in the kitchen.

1 package frozen puff pastry. (Or use Sue's Pie Crust Recipe)
1 pound Jimmy Dean sage pork sausage
½ medium onion, chopped fine
1 egg, beaten

Preheat oven to 400° F

Roll out the puff pastry to 8" by 20"
Mix the onion into the sausage, then cut the sausage in half and roll each half to a 20" roll. Place flour in your hands to prevent the sausage from sticking.
Lay the sausage you have just rolled on top of the pastry in the center. Roll the pastry around the sausage tube. Brush water on the edges of the pastry then overlap the edges. Seal the ends together with your fingers. Brush the top of the pastry with the beaten egg. Cut the long roll into 2½ " slices and make a couple little diagonal cuts on top of each roll with a sharp knife. Bake on a broiling pan covered with tinfoil. Make cuts into the foil to allow the grease from the sausage to drip below.

Bake for 20 to 25 minutes until the rolls puff up and are lightly brown. Remove from pan and place on paper towels to absorb excess grease.

Scotch Eggs

This is a wonderful savory dish. Once you have tried them at your High Tea, it will be a favorite. The combination of sausage and eggs in a new presentation is always fun to try. My mother made this recipe by frying them. This one, by baking, is much quicker… and eliminates many calories!

1-pound pork sausage
1 Tablespoon fresh chopped chives or green onion.
Salt and pepper to taste
12 small hard boiled eggs, peeled
Flour for coating
2 eggs, beaten
1 ½ cups breadcrumbs

Mix sausage, chives, salt, and pepper.
Divide into 12 portions. On a floured surface, flatten sausage mixture into a round circle. Dust eggs with flour. Place beaten eggs into a small bowl and the breadcrumbs into another bowl. Place each egg on a circle of sausage; mold the sausage around the egg, sealing seams well with water. Roll each sausage-covered egg in beaten egg, then into the breadcrumbs. Place onto a cookie sheet.

Bake the eggs in the oven at 400° F for 30 minutes or until sausage is well done. Drain onto the paper towel. To prevent the eggs from rolling on the baking sheet, place a toothpick through the bottom of the eggs at an angle.

Toad In the Hole

Don't let this old English name discourage you from trying this tasty and easy dish. My mother made this often for our tea (supper) when we were growing up. You should have seen our friends' faces when we told them the menu!

1-1/2 pounds link sausage (try low-fat)
2 eggs
1 cup flour
1/2 teaspoon salt
1/4 teaspoon pepper
2 cups milk

Brown the sausages and place them in an oblong 11 x 7 greased baking dish. Place the sausage links evenly apart in the pan, so the batter can go between the sausages. Mix the eggs, flour, salt, pepper, and milk, mix well with a rotary beater or whisk, and pour over the sausage. As it bakes, the "heads" of some of the sausage will poke up through the batter. Bake for 30 minutes.

Scottish Stovies

This traditional British recipe is a great way to use up leftover roast beef. I have had many variations, but this is my favorite. Serve with Beer Bread and a salad for a very quick meal.

6 slices chopped bacon
2 pounds potatoes, scrubbed and chopped
1 large onion, chopped
1 large carrot, chopped
8 ounces of beef or vegetable stock
Salt and pepper to taste
Chopped left-over roast beef
1 Tablespoon Worcestershire sauce
Grated sharp cheddar cheese

Cook bacon in frying pan until slightly curled. Add the onions and fry until golden. Add the potatoes, carrots and the stock. Cook, covered, until tender, about 20 to 25 minutes. Add the beef and Worcestershire sauce and mix well. Turn into a greased casserole dish, top with the cheese and place under the broiler until the cheese is bubbly and beginning to turn brown. Watch closely, as the cheese can burn quickly.

Cottage Pie

Here is a recipe that is simple and good. My British friend Margaret gave me this timesaving recipe. It is very similar to Shepherd's Pie. This can also be made with leftover roast beef, cut into small pieces, instead of the ground beef. In England, hamburger or ground meat is called minced beef.

1 pound lean ground beef
1 medium onion, chopped
6 medium to large carrots, peeled and chopped
1/2 teaspoon Marmite or Vegemite (this is optional, but can be found in specialty stores)
1/3 cup tomato paste
1 vegetable or beef bouillon cube, dissolved in 1/4 cup boiling water
4 ounces chopped tomatoes (can use canned)
Salt and pepper to taste
4 cups mashed potatoes (previously cooked and warmed)

In a frying pan, brown the onions until soft, not browned. Add ground beef and brown with the onions until beef turns brown. Add carrots, Marmite, tomato paste, bouillon, tomatoes, salt, and pepper. Simmer for 1/2 hour, and then place into a greased casserole dish.

Mash the potatoes with a little milk to make them soft. Place the mashed potatoes on top of the beef mixture and bake at 300° F for 15 minutes. Sprinkle some grated Parmesan cheese on top and broil until light brown.

SCONES AND BREADS
The scones for high tea should be less sweet and more of a savory scone. You won't serve Devonshire cream with these scones, just butter and jam. Choose one that will compliment your savory course.

Irish Potato Scones

Instead of serving the scones with Devonshire cream and jam, use butter and jam.

    2 cups flour
    1 teaspoon cream of tartar
    1 teaspoon baking soda
    1/2 teaspoon salt
    2 teaspoons sugar
    1/2 cup butter, softened
    1/4 cup cold mashed potatoes (made without butter or milk)
    3/4 cup milk or buttermilk
    Cream for topping

Sift the dry ingredients into a large bowl, then cut in the butter and potatoes with a pastry blender or cutter. Stir in the flour, then add the milk and mix gently. If dough is too sticky, add more flour.

Place dough onto lightly floured surface and pat to 3/4 inch thick. Cut with a cookie cutter into desired shapes (dip the cutter into the flour after each use). Brush tops lightly with cream. Bake on ungreased cookie sheet for 12 to 15 minutes at 400° F.

Cheese Scones

Scones that aren't so sweet go best with High Tea.
With this easy recipe, you'll have hot, delicious scones ready in minutes.

2 cups Original Bisquick brand mix
1/3 cup sharp cheddar cheese, shredded
3 Tablespoons sugar
1/3 cup whipping (heavy) cream
1 egg
2 Tablespoons milk
2 Tablespoons sugar

Heat oven to 425°F. Grease a cookie sheet.

Mix Bisquick, cheese, sugar, whipping cream, and egg until soft dough forms. Turn the dough onto lightly floured surface. Roll the dough into the flour to coat. Shape the dough into a ball and knead gently 8 to 10 times.

Flour hands and pat dough into an 8-inch circle on cookie sheet. Brush dough with milk; sprinkle with 2 Tablespoons sugar. Cut into 8 wedges, but do not separate.

Bake at 425° F about 12 minutes or until golden brown; carefully separate wedges. Serve warm.

Honey Scones

2-1/3 cups all purpose flour
1/3 cup sugar
2-½ teaspoons baking powder
¼ teaspoon salt
½ cup butter
1/3 cup honey
½ cup whipping cream

Preheat oven to 350° F

Grease a baking sheet

Combine flour, sugar, baking powder, and salt. Using a pastry blender or cutter, cut in the butter until the mixture is crumbly.

In another bowl, combine the honey and half of the whipping cream, then add to the butter mixture and stir until all dry ingredients are coated and moistened.

Roll or pat out the dough on a lightly floured surface until the dough is ½-inch thick. Use a round cookie cutter or biscuit cutter and cut out the scones and place on the greased baking sheet. Brush the tops of the scones with a small amount of whipping cream and sprinkle with sugar.

Bake for 18 to 20 minutes until the scones are lightly browned. Serve with butter and preserves.

Beer or Ale Bread

This quick and easy bread goes nicely with Scotch eggs.

3 cups self-rising flour
¼ cup sugar
1 12-ounce beer - room temperature
½ cup melted butter

If you do not have self-rising flour, substitute the following:
3 cups flour
4-½ teaspoons baking powder
½ teaspoon salt

Preheat oven to 375° F

Mix the dry ingredients with beer and pour into a greased loaf pan. Pour the melted butter on top of the mixture.
Bake for one hour and remove from pan. Cool for at least 10 to 15 minutes before cutting. Serve with butter and enjoy.

Irish Soda Bread

4 cups flour
1-½ teaspoons salt
1 teaspoon baking soda
1 Tablespoon baking powder
2 Tablespoons sugar
¼ cup butter
2 cups buttermilk
1 egg

¼ cup currants (optional)

Preheat oven to 375° F
Grease a cookie sheet

Mix the flour, salt, baking soda, baking powder, and sugar in a large bowl. Cut in the butter that has been cut into small pieces with a pastry blender/cutter until the mixture is like coarse crumbs.
In a smaller bowl, beat the egg and the buttermilk together, then add this mixture to the bowl of dry ingredients and mix into a dough. If adding currants, stir them in at this time.
Knead the dough on a lightly floured surface several times. Divide the dough into two halves and form into round loaves. Place both loaves onto the baking sheet and with a sharp knife, cut a cross into the top of each loaf.

Bake for about 35 to 40 minutes.
The loaves should sound hollow when you thump them.

Remove from oven and place on a wire rack.
Brush tops with a small amount of melted butter.
Slice and enjoy.

Crumpets

We have all heard the expression, "tea and crumpets", usually associated with British literature! They are also very tasty at high tea. Butter, jam, and lemon curd, are the perfect companions. These are best serve toasted and warm. You can make crumpets with an English muffin ring or a cleaned tuna can with the top and bottom removed for the baking ring. Crumpets are not the same as an English muffin. Crumpets have a slightly spongy texture with a holey top which absorbs toppings very well. They are not cut in half as are English muffins.

3 ½ cups flour
2 Tablespoons butter, melted
2 teaspoons salt
2 teaspoons sugar
2 ½ teaspoons dry yeast
1 cup warm water
1 cup warm whole milk
½ teaspoons baking soda dissolved in ¼ cup warm water

1. Stir together the yeast and the water and let stand for 5 to 10 minutes. Add the warm milk, butter, sugar and salt. Then add the flour and stir just until the batter becomes smooth. Let this sit for 25 to 30 minutes.
2. Stir in the soda mixture and let this rise for 20 to 30 minutes.
3. Heat the griddle over medium heat and grease. Place the crumpet rings on the griddle for just a minute, then pour batter into the rings. Lower the heat to a low setting, cover the griddle and cook the crumpets until the tops are holey and dry, about 8 to 10 minutes.
4. Flip over the crumpet rings and cook for a few more minutes. Remove carefully from the rings. Serve warm.

Desserts or Puddings

A high tea can also include some assorted cheeses, crackers, and sliced fruit, served in place of dessert. The cheese, crackers, and fruit could also be served with the savory course. Some of these desserts are also a wonderful addition to a dinner party. I thought you would enjoy them even if you are not having a high tea.

English Trifle

When I was a child, we begged mother to make this trifle. It is not the traditional trifle that you might have made before, but it's the perfect ending to a High Tea.

1 large package Jell-O, any flavor, made as directed on package – do not set.
1 large package vanilla pudding or Bird's English Custard, made as directed on package.
1 angel food cake or sponge cake.
1 large can fruit cocktail, drained.
2 cups whipping cream, whipped.
Maraschino cherries for garnish.

Cut cake into 1-inch squares and place them in the bottom of a trifle bowl. Pour liquid Jell-O over the cake pieces, followed by the fruit cocktail, and blend very gently. Refrigerate until the Jell-O is set. Spread cooled custard or pudding over Jell-O combination, and top with the whipped cream. Decorate with the cherries.

Lemon Coconut Poppy Seed Cake

Our friend John won't come to tea unless I bake this cake! This is also a nice cake to keep on hand if just serving it with a cup of tea. Can you imagine the commotion in the kitchen at Downton Abbey *if Mrs. Patmore was presented with the option of any kind of a cake mix?*

1 package lemon cake mix
1 small package instant lemon pudding mix (not sugar-free)
1 cup sour cream
1/2 cup oil
4 eggs
1/2 cup water
1 teaspoon coconut extract (add to water)
1/3 cup poppy seeds

Preheat oven to 350° F
Grease a Bundt pan thoroughly with baking cooking spray or cooking spray and floured.

Mix the cake mix, pudding mix, sour cream, oil, eggs, water, and coconut extract in large mixing bowl, then beat on medium speed for 2 minutes. Fold in poppy seeds, and pour into prepared Bundt pan.

Bake at 350° F for 50 to 60 minutes.

Cool in pan for 15 minutes, then place cake upside down on cake plate.

Dust with powdered sugar, slice, and serve when cool. Add some fresh raspberries for an added treat.

Rachel's Sticky Toffee Pudding

Another favorite! This recipe is said to have started in the Lake District in England. I am sure it would have been a favorite of the Downton Abbey *staff. This recipe is from my cousin Rachel, who is the founder and owner of The Pudding Kitchen in Somerset, England (ThePuddingKitchen.co.uk). She is a gourmet cook and anything she makes is wonderful. You will love this recipe and it may very well become your favorite, as it is mine.*

1-1/3 cups chopped dates
¾ cup boiling water
1-1/3 cup self-rising flour
1 teaspoon baking soda
2 eggs
1/3 cup butter
¾ cup brown sugar
2 Tablespoons molasses (Treacle if in England)
1/3 cup milk

Toffee Sauce
¾ cup brown sugar (or muscovado - available-from Whole Foods)
3 ½ Tablespoons butter
1 cup heavy whipping cream
1 Tablespoon molasses

Pour boiling water over the dates and let soak for 30 minutes.

Preheat oven to 325° F

Butter and flour 6 small custard cups and place on a baking sheet.
Beat butter and sugar together until creamy. Gradually add the eggs, and then the molasses to the butter and sugar. Mix the flour and the baking

soda together with a whisk, then fold half of the flour mixture into the butter and sugar, then half the milk, and repeat. Stir in the soaked dates to the batter. Spoon the mixture into the custard cups equally. Bake for 20 to 25 minutes until risen and firm to the touch. Remove from oven and place baking sheet on wire rack.

While the puddings are baking, make the toffee sauce:
Place the butter, sugar and half of the cream into a pan and gradually bring to a boil, stirring constantly until sugar has dissolved. Stir in the molasses and bring back to a boil for a couple of minutes to get a rich toffee color. Stir continually to prevent burning.

Remove from heat and stir in the remaining whipping cream. Turn the puddings into individual serving bowls and pour the sauce over each pudding. Serve while sauce is warm, or reheat for about 15 minutes, covered with foil.

British Bread and Butter Pudding

This is an old and traditional dessert that has its origins from the 1700s and was a staple in every English kitchen, even Downton Abbey's. *It is baked in the oven and then served with or without a sauce. You can use any kind of day-old bread (I like to use baguettes as it absorbs the egg-milk mixture much better). It is a great way to use up left over bread. This pudding is such a comfort food, both to body and spirit, a classic British favorite.*

½ cup of sultanas or raisins
2 Tablespoons brandy (optional)
5 eggs
2-2/3 cups half-and-half
1/3 cup sugar
1 orange, grated rind only
1 teaspoon vanilla
½ teaspoon cinnamon
8 thick slices of day old bread, buttered and cut into cubes
¼ cup butter
1 Tablespoon powdered sugar

Combine the sultanas and the brandy in a small bowl and set aside. Combine the eggs, half-and-half, sugar, orange rind, vanilla and cinnamon in bowl and whisk to combine.

Place the sultanas into the bottom of a greased oval baking dish. Place buttered bread cubes on top of the sultanas. Pour the cream and egg mixture over the bread cubes and let stand until completely absorbed moisture, at least one hour or refrigerated overnight. Preheat oven to 350°F and bake until golden and the egg mixture is firm, 30 to 40 minutes. Lightly dust with powdered sugar. Serve warm with or without sauce.

Sauce for Bread and Butter Pudding

4 eggs
½ cup sugar
¼ teaspoon salt
2 ½ cups milk
1 ½ teaspoon vanilla

Beat the eggs, sugar and salt in a medium heavy pan until well blended, then stir in the milk. Cook over low heat, stirring constantly until mixture is thick enough to coat a metal spoon, about 15 minutes. Do not boil. Remove from heat and cool for a few minutes, then stir in the vanilla. Serve warm. If not serving right away, cover with a piece of plastic wrap to prevent a film from forming on top. Refrigerate. For a quick sauce you can also use Bird's English Custard Powder. This can be purchased at any grocery store. Just mix with milk and follow the directions.

"She found a cloth and laid the tea, setting out cakes and biscuits, sugar bowl and silver milk jug. Even for kitchen tea, it appeared, her standards were meticulous."

ROSAMUNDE PILCHER. *"THE DAY OF THE STORM"*

CHAPTER 5

The Manners and Etiquette of Tea Time

• • •

"Manners are a sensitive awareness of the feelings of others. If you have
that awareness, you have good manners, no matter what fork you use."

- EMILY POST

ETIQUETTE AND GOOD MANNERS, MORE than anything else, help others feel
comfortable. With the addition of social networking and technology to
our society, we are faced with the need for updated information on correct etiquette. For several years I have pondered this situation, and realized that manners have not changed over the past century. During the
Edwardian era, the years of *Downton Abbey* and the *Titanic*, good manners
were the expected behavior of all people, especially the upper class.

"Society is like a convention, a town meeting, a trades union, a caucus. Did
it not have certain rules it would relapse into chaos, and those rules are, by
common consent, called by one generic term – Etiquette." Etiquette, The
American Code of Manners, by Mrs. M.E.W. Sherwood, 1884.

Since our lifestyles are very different than those of our ancestors, we tend to think it stodgy and outdated to worry about manners and etiquette. However, statistics show that even though a prospective employee is qualified and friendly, the candidate with good manners is most likely to be given the new job. Most people think manners and etiquette are only for the wealthy or the "country club set", but good manners and etiquette are for everyone. Since the release of my last book *First-Class Etiquette*, I have been asked on numerous occasions to give classes to high school and college-age students. Many mothers tell me they wished they had not been so lax in the earlier years of their children's lives.

Children in the Edwardian era were taught to speak when spoken to. Table manners were impeccable; if not, the children were asked to leave the table. Manners were an important part of everyday life, and an accurate indication of one's status in society. Proper manners told the world if you were from "downstairs or upstairs." How one ate, spoke, dressed, and sat were a tell-tale sign of breeding or one's place in society. On the set of *Downton Abbey*, Alastair Bruce, an expert on Edwardian and historical etiquette, advises the cast on proper manners and etiquette of that era. It's a modern group of actors and actresses that star in *Downton Abbey* and times have changed; life is more relaxed. It was a constant task while filming to keep everyone sitting up straight at the table, as dining today is more informal and casual than it was in 1912.

In our modern world, manners and proper etiquette still have their places. It is important today, as it was for the family and staff of *Downton Abbey* and the passengers and crew of the *Titanic*, to realize that manners matter. It was, and still is, a common courtesy, to be kind and respectful to one another, and to apply the "Golden Rule" in all situations. We just need to remember to have fun, but still behave!

So, in everything, do to others what you would have them do to you.

MATTHEW 7:12 NIV

While writing my children's book *First-Class Etiquette*, whenever I was dining in a restaurant, I kept an eye out for children with good table manners. Unfortunately, this was not usually the case. This saddened me. My hope is that this book will encourage readers to apply some of my suggestions to their families.

The family of today eats on the run, and it is the exception rather than the rule for the family to have dinner together. More relaxed dining habits have resulted in more requests for manners and etiquette classes. Young people with good manners and etiquette skills are at an advantage when entering the business and social worlds. It was unusual for children of the Edwardian era to leave home without knowing how to behave in public.

Good manners never go out of style. The opportunity to instill good manners in a child needs to start early in life. Parents and grandparents are the obvious role models for good manners. We can't have two sets of manners, one for home and one for use in public; but sadly that is exactly what we see today. If we want good manners for our children, we must practice good manners ourselves. Fred Astaire stated, "The hardest job kids face today is learning good manners without seeing any."

Of what I observe, I am not completely innocent. I have picked up fast food for my children and grandchildren at a drive through on the way to a soccer game or football practice. I have skipped a sit-down meal with my husband in place of a meal in front of the computer while writing this book. However, I find that when I make time for manners, manners give me more time – more time for the important things. Manners offer the perfect opportunity to "disconnect." When I put down my phone at dinner, I get to spend more quality time with a loved one over a delicious meal. When I schedule in extra time for dinner at a table rather than in the car, I am able to slow down and appreciate the intricate process of nourishing my body. Also, we may miss important cues from our body, like "I am hungry, or I am full" if we are speeding off to our next obligation. I am always trying to practice what I preach and I want to share insights that have value for others.

One of the best places to start practicing good manners is family dinners at home. As a nation, we seem to be in the car a great deal of time, driving to music lessons, soccer, and football practice. A whole generation of children now think it's normal to consume fast-food meals in the car or in front of the television. Start with one night a week. All members of the family should sit at the table, talk about their day, and enjoy a meal together. It may sound radical to some families, but there's no place like home to begin.

A study by the University of Minnesota found that having a habit of shared family meals improves nutrition, academic performance, interpersonal skills, and reduces the risk of eating disorders. Other studies cite research that teenagers who often eat dinner with their families are less likely to drink, smoke, or use drugs.

I was born in England and have been involved in the business of tea for many years, and my inclination is to present etiquette and manners from the "tea-table" point of view. However, tea manners and etiquette are really the same as manners and etiquette for any dining situation. The following guidelines for dining at the tea table are interchangeable with the dinner table.

ETIQUETTE TIPS FOR TEA-TIME AND THE DINNER TABLE

* Having to listen to others' conversations while they talk on cell phones is becoming habitual and annoying. It is not uncommon these days to see business establishments place a sign in the entrance: "No Cell Phones, Please." Cell phones should be turned off before taking your place at the table. This is proper etiquette for any meal, and, of course, for afternoon tea. Purses, glasses, keys, lipstick, and cell phones should never be placed on the table, but under your chair, or better yet left with your coat.

* Several hundred years ago, teacups had no handles. The Chinese were among the first to drink tea that they consumed from a bowl rather than a teacup. Therefore, without a handle, it was natural to extend one's pinkie finger to balance the cup when drinking. Since the little and ring fingers are more sensitive to heat, this also was a way to keep from burning one's fingers. Now that teacups have handles, it is considered a "faux pas" to raise your pinkie finger when drinking tea.

* Always say "Please" and Thank you" when asking for something to be passed or when you receive an item or service.

* Stir quietly - the teaspoon should not hit against the inside of your cup. Imagine the clatter if everyone were to clink their teacups at the same time.

* When finished stirring your sugar or milk into your tea, place the used teaspoon behind your cup on the saucer. The spoon should never be placed again on the tablecloth.

* If you have used a tea bag to make tea, don't place the tea bag on the saucer. A small dish should be provided to hold the used tea bag.

* When dining out, if you are served a teapot with hot water in it, and teabags, the teabag should always go into the teapot, not into the cup.

- When serving condiments for your scone, place the jam or clotted cream onto your plate, not directly onto your scone. When eating your scone, break off a small piece and place a small amount of jam and cream onto the scone and eat. If you cut your scone in half, never place the two halves back together after adding jam or cream.
- Do not eat your scone with a fork.
- Gloves must always be removed for eating. Hats may remain in place if a veil is not covering the face.
- When sitting 12 inches or less from a table, only the teacup is lifted and the saucer is left on the table. If sitting in a living room, and using a coffee table, the saucer and cup are lifted together from the table. The left hand should hold the saucer and the right hand should hold the cup while drinking the tea. The teacup should rest on the saucer when not drinking tea. This is also the proper etiquette if you are standing and drinking tea.
- While drinking tea from the cup, don't look into the cup, but at those around you.
- Keep your elbows off the table at all times.
- Leave your plate in its position when you are finished eating. Do not push it away.
- Wait for the hostess to begin eating before you begin to eat.
- When your hostess and host place their napkins in their laps, that's your clue for doing the same.
- Use your napkin to blot your mouth, not to blot your lipstick.
- Avoid burping or making other rude noises at the table.
- Eat slowly and chew with your mouth closed.
- Always use the sugar tongs, never your finger, to pick up sugar cubes.
- Teacups and saucers should be placed at the 2 o'clock position relative to the plate. The handles of the cups should always be at a right angle and pointed to 4 o'clock with the teaspoon at a right

angle behind the cup. This will make your tea table look proper and organized.

- If you desire to use milk in your tea, never use half-and-half, cream, or cream-substitute coffee flavorings. Use whole milk or 2 per cent milk as it gives the tea a rich flavor; non-fat can give it a chalky look.
- Lemons should be in small wedges and served with a fork. It is best to remove the lemon wedges before drinking the tea. If using lemon, do not add milk to your tea, because it will curdle.
- Are you a Miffy or a Tiffy? A Miffy (milk in first) puts the milk into the cup before pouring the tea, and a Tiffy (tea in first) pours the tea into the cup then adds the milk. Mr. Samuel H. G. Twining, ninth-generation director of Twinings Tea, gave a tea presentation at the Bath Spa Hotel in Bath, England, attended by my cousin Angela. His advice was contrary to many tea "experts" who insist the tea is poured first. Mr. Twinning stated it is correct is to add the milk first!
- Serving tea: You, as the hostess, should pour everyone's tea. Never pass the teapot around the table; in Victorian times, this was considered being the "Mum." However, if you have eight or more guests for tea, it is a great honor to ask a dear friend if she would help pour the tea. (Mum: asking a close friend to do the honors of serving tea.)
- When pouring tea for your guests, make sure the teacup and saucer are sitting on the table, not held up in the air. You will avoid burning someone if you follow this tip.
- Never fill the teacup to the rim. It could easily spill over into the saucer and cause the teacup to drip while drinking.

Etiquette is a customary code of polite behavior in society. It is showing good taste, kindness, and consideration to others. In our world of casual and lackadaisical living, almost anything goes. This is all the more reason for taking the time to prepare and serve others with the traditional refinements of culture and respect. Etiquette will always be the model for good living. This has not changed and will never change.

Bruce Richardson, a historian and tea expert says, "Americans in the Ritz's tea room stand out because they work so hard to keep their pinkies extended while holding their teacup. It makes you look pretentious. If you pay attention to your manners, put the napkin in your lap, and keep your feet off the table, you'll probably be OK."

George Washington even had something to say about manners: "Every action done in the company of others ought to be done with some sign of respect to those that are present."

While we don't have the strict confinements that were in vogue during the *Downton Abbey* and *Titanic* era, we have a legacy of politeness and tradition that carries into all areas of life. Manners are to show respect, not about being pretentious. We can thank those from the earlier generations who left us guidelines for dining etiquette and consideration for others.

"You can get through life with bad manners,
but it's easier with good manners."

- LILLIAN GISH

CHAPTER 6

The Gift of Hospitality

• • •

*"The focus of entertaining is impressing
others; the focus of true hospitality
is serving others."*

- TIM CHESTER

OUR SEVEN GRANDDAUGHTERS LOVE AFTERNOON tea. When they were very young, we enjoyed teatime using an old wicker basket transformed into a tea hamper. I lined the interior of this hinged-lid basket with a Laura Ashley-type fabric, and placed antique pictures of teapots and teacups on the lid. Inside were tea accouterments, vintage hankies that doubled as napkins, decorated sugar cubes, several kinds of tea, and shortbread cookies. When the girls arrived, the hamper was ready.

Tea was served in the garden under a tree, at the dining room table, or during the winter months on a quilt in front of the fireplace. Many precious memories exist from those sweet visits.

Granddaughters as guests provide the purest form of hospitality. No pretense, no need to impress; it was a place of love, comfort, and acceptance. We put on "airs', we laughed, we dined, and sometimes we wore hats, gloves, and fancy dress-up clothes, but most of all, we enjoyed one another. This was effortless hospitality, spending time with those we love and having fun.

The concept of hospitality is not new to me. My mother was the "Queen" of hospitality. Our front door was always open and when friends arrived unannounced mother put the kettle on. She could also just as easily set the table with china and candlesticks, add a vase of fresh flowers, and serve a four-course meal with little notice. Our home was a place for folks to gather, formally or informally, and food was the medium that brought it all together. My fondest memories as a child are around the table…a dinner table, a picnic table or a tea table.

My mother's home in England was very formal, but it was a haven to "old age pensioners" (senior citizens). She and her older sister Olive spent many of their summer holidays at the seaside, providing a getaway for the elderly. Monday mornings, my grandfather would drive the 50 miles in his cherished 1930 Model A Ford to the lovely seaside village of Heacham, where he and my grandmother had a roomy and white-washed, clapboard cottage. Four or five elderly ladies (or gentlemen) were delighted to be chosen to spend time in the family cottage by the sea. The guests would have several days to bask in the sunshine, walk on the beach, or just lounge on deck chairs and read. Weather permitting, afternoon tea was served on my grandmother's china on the porch. My mother and Olive entertained the guests by playing cards and games with them, then doubled as cooks and maids to assist my grandmother.

On Friday after lunch, my grandfather would drive the guests home. Four of them would squeeze into the back seat and one lucky soul would sit up front with my grandfather. Their luggage would be stowed in the travel trunk mounted on the rear of the car. On Monday, the week started over again with four or five new guests coming for a seaside holiday.

Years later, walking on that same beach, near my grandparent's English cottage, I imagined the delight and joy those dear souls received. I am so grateful for the legacy of hospitality passed down from my grandparents and their daughters.

Author's family enjoying afternoon tea in the garden.
England - Circa 1915.

Hospitality at *Downton Abbey* (or on the *Titanic*) might appear stiff and formal, but the attention to detail was for a desired result. Guests were given the highest priority. Their comfort and pleasure were of utmost importance, and the service from the staff was a reflection of the host family's standing in the community or the ships distinction for excellence. As a meal or tea was served, the guests were provided with the little extras to help them feel at home. Protocol was of the utmost importance and most of the guests were of the social class to know the expected decorum.

Downstairs, it was more hustle and bustle. Invariably a bell would ring summoning one of the staff to run upstairs for the Crawley family during mealtime. The evening meal for the servants, high tea, was served early before the family's formal dinner. The table setting and food for the staff was very informal. Mrs. Patmore, the cook in *Downton Abbey* and her kitchen staff prepared meals for the servants and the family, then would eat when everyone had been served. Nothing was left to chance. Preparations for meals and the comfort of the guests would be of the highest consideration. Mrs. Hughes, the housekeeper in *Downton Abbey*, had utmost authority to make sure rooms were prepared and meals served promptly. Nothing was missing in a guest's bedroom, or at the dinner table.

Social class does not define hospitality. The needs of others is the main concern. While *Downton Abbey* is focused on the eating and drinking habits of the upper-class Edwardian household, hospitality never goes out of style. It provides the true purpose of opening our homes and offering a place of refuge.

Inviting others into our homes is an enjoyable and relaxed way to spend time with friends. The setting provides privacy and comfort not found in restaurants or hotels. Whether small and cozy, or large and luxurious, our homes are gifts to us from God. We are His servants and the joy that we can give others by using our homes is the basic concept of hospitality. The very word "hospitality" means "hospice," which is a place of shelter and healing. Serving others is not a new concept. It implies using my gift of "hospitality" by serving a meal or offering a place to stay. Some homes have an "open door policy", where friends are welcome anytime; some more formal - invitations are issued before the welcome mat is extended.

Personal preferences will dictate our style, but our gift for making others feel comfortable is part of hospitality. We may not have the time or funds to have the perfect house, perfect meal, or perfect afternoon tea, but it's exciting to share our homes and offer comfort and healing to all that enter.

A few years ago, I was asked to participate in a "mini-retreat" at our church. The day was planned for women in our church and community to participate in workshops on a variety of topics: quilting, gardening, antiques, writing, sewing, and hospitality. I gave the workshop on hospitality. Since I had years of experience preparing afternoon teas for many occasions, my presentation was "The Art of Afternoon Tea." Both my mother and I thought it was rather a silly idea to be teaching women to make tea, and I didn't expect more than 25 ladies to attend the workshop. Imagine our surprise when the final count was 150! The event became two workshops with 75 ladies in each class. Two dear friends volunteered to help serve tea and bake cookies. A Sunday school classroom was converted into a delightful tearoom, complete with posters of the English countryside, a teacart, tea books, tea lamps, and many teapots and teacups. Each lady brought her own teacup, as there would be no drinking tea out of Styrofoam cups.

The mini-retreat was the beginning of a new career for me, as I was invited to share at various women's events. My passion became a ministry that now reaches more women than I could have imagined.

I encourage and educate others how to open their homes and use their gifts of hospitality. Tea is just a tool to share our gifts. I am always surprised that the idea is so foreign to so many women of all ages. More surprising is the fear so many woman face in "having company." It may be that the influence of wealth in the media gives us the apprehension of not having the proper dishes, furniture, or even thinking our homes aren't nice enough to entertain. The Bible tells us that hospitality is important to God. It doesn't mention all the unease we have, but just encourages us to practice hospitality. Hospitality is not an option or a suggestion. Pretty strong words, but true.

Entertaining and hospitality are similar words, but very different in meaning. I have spent a lot of time trying to define the distinction between those two words, as many women have confused them and talked themselves out of a blessing. Webster's Dictionary doesn't provide much difference between the two, but when comparing the words with the action involved, there *is* a distinction. Entertaining is a form of amusing, keeping busy for the sake of having something to do. Hospitality is taking on a servant's heart, giving to others without ever expecting anything in return.

Welcoming guests into our homes and giving them a warm reception is something anyone can accomplish. The increase of magazines on the newsstands about home decorating and entertaining are indicators that women really do want to use their homes.

The photographs on the glossy covers of those magazines promise the same look in your home. My home will never look like that! Many of you might feel the same. That's the point! Hospitality is reaching out and serving those whom God puts in our path, not having the Taj Mahal as our homes. Visual or culinary charm is not the object; it's all about helping hearts to connect.

Meeting the need for food and shelter in the life of others has always been a very practical way to obey God. In the Old Testament, Abraham knew his reputation was on the line if he neglected to treat the three men who appeared at his tent unannounced. In Genesis 18:1-8, Abraham and his wife Sarah prepared a place for the men to rest, took care of their physical needs, and prepared food. Little did they know that the three men were actually angels who had come to bear the news that Sarah and Abraham would have a child. (At age 90 and 100!) What a blessing they would have missed if they had failed to show hospitality.

> *"Do not forget to show hospitality to strangers, for by so doing some people have shown hospitality to angels without knowing it."*

> HEBREWS 13:2 NIV

Wonderful ideas for decorating and recipes for food preparation can be gleaned from the numerous magazines available, but the model for hospitality is the Word of God. Entertaining seeks repayment, a return invitation, with each successive party outdoing the last. But hospitality is the joy of serving where we are, with what we have, with no thought of repayment.

Give yourself permission to have guests in your home. Prepare a dinner or an afternoon tea with no thought of being perfect. Just do the best you can, not in competition with magazines, neighbors, or friends. Whatever the setting, a clean house, a dirty house, a small apartment, a luxurious large home, at a park, or at the beach, the true essence of hosting an afternoon tea party or a meal, is the hospitality extended.

> *"Tea is the ultimate form of hospitality."*

> - AMY VANDERBILT

CHAPTER 7

The Pleasures of Tea

• • •

Celebrating Among Friends

"Tea urges tranquility of the soul."

- William Wordsworth Longfellow

Most cruise ships and luxury hotels offer afternoon tea, and depending on the registry of the ship, it might be an authentic tea in all details. A proper English Afternoon Tea consists of small crust-less tea sandwiches, scones served with jam and Devonshire cream, sweets, pastries, and the faithful pot of hot tea. The importance of tea during the Victorian and Edwardian eras made afternoon tea a high priority both at *Downton Abbey* and on the *Titanic*.

Creating an afternoon tea in your home will let you partake in what many women of the early 1900s experienced when they practiced hospitality. Keep in mind that many of those women had butlers who served the tea, cooks who prepared the tea, and housekeepers who cleaned the house! While Mrs. Patmore, the cook in *Downton Abbey*, enjoyed her tea at the large farmhouse table in the kitchen, she also had spent hours preparing the elegant tea being enjoyed upstairs.

Tea was an integral part of the culture of those days, as it still is in England. Increasingly, Americans are regaining an interest in and awareness of the soothing social occasion of afternoon tea. *Downton Abbey* and *Titanic* teas are cropping up all over the country. It is interesting to view the menus and see pictures of the attendees dressing in the clothing of that era.

I am always on the lookout for clothing and hats to wear when I appear at book signings or speak to groups about the Edwardian times. I have collected china like that used on the set of *Downton Abbey*, and have received gifts of replica teacups from the *Titanic*, complete with the White Star insignia. Using these delightful pieces of china adds to the ambience of having tea in the early 19th century.

Creating a tea event for friends and family in your home will give you a delightful sense of pleasure as you continue a practice that has been a custom for generations. While preparing for tea, you might discover the joy of using your grandmother's teapot, drinking tea from your mother's morning teacup, or using some of the vintage linens hand-embroidered by an auntie. If this is a new venture for you, plan on having great adventures scouring flea markets and antique shops to find just the right items you need for teatime.

The art of afternoon tea is nothing more than having a plan and then following through. It involves time and work, but you will love the rewards. My mother used to say, "Do what you can, where you are, with what you have." This takes the pressure off your need to perform, and allows you to be involved in the joy of making your guests feel at home, and sharing a tradition that can be as grand and resplendent as if you were having tea at *Downton Abbey* or on the decks or saloons of the *Titanic*.

There are three variations of the English tea party: Traditional Afternoon Tea; Cream Tea; and High Tea. The most popular is the **Traditional Afternoon Tea,** which consists of savories (tea sandwiches), scones with jam and Devonshire cream, and sweets and desserts. This is usually served between 3 p.m. and 5 p.m. It is rather formal in nature, protocol, and etiquette prevailing. Another tea is the **Cream Tea.** This is less formal and much easier to prepare, as it consists of scones with jam and Devonshire cream, and a pot of tea. It is also served in the afternoon. Many people believe that **High Tea** is a regal and fancy tea, but in reality it is the least elaborate of the three teas. Many tearooms, hotels, and cruise ships advertise High Tea as an elegant and posh tea, but the only thing "high" about this tea is the price. It is the same thing as supper for most of the average folks or working-class in England and America.

By the way, some people believe that the term "posh," the state of being elegant, stylish, or upper-class, was formed from the initials of Portside Out, Starboard Home, referring to the practice of the wealthy, especially those exposed to the sun on voyages between England and India., choosing their accommodations on ships.

Thousands of pieces of china, silver, and fine dining items were testimony of the fact that everything to the last detail was done right on the *Titanic*. It was common knowledge that the White Star Line was the "top of the line" when it came to passenger accommodations.

All three classes of passengers were served tea, although in the different variations. Third-class, or steerage, passengers were not accustomed to stopping in the middle of the afternoon for a three-course tea, so a pot of tea and cookies, or biscuits as they are called in England, were provided for them in either of two dining rooms located on the F deck.

Second-class passengers had their afternoon tea in the beautiful library, with almost the same tea as that served to the First-class passengers, since the main kitchen served both classes.

The wealthiest people in the world dressed in the latest fashion for afternoon tea in First-class. They were served tea in one of several locations that provided very cozy atmospheres for afternoon tea. The Veranda Café, separate from the main area of the ship, had large windows, palm trees and ivy, and comfortable wicker furniture - a charming and elegant place for afternoon tea for the rich and famous.

The menus and food for all passengers were far superior on the White Star Lines than other ships of that time. First-class passengers also had the luxury of having an additional dining option, the a' la Carte dining room. It provided a remarkable resemblance to dining at the Ritz in London. Its head chef, Luigi Gatti, was hired from the famous hotel; and the owner of the Ritz, Cesar Ritz, trained the *Titanic's* restaurant staff. I have enjoyed afternoon tea at the Ritz in London where it is an exceptional event, so there is little doubt that the afternoon tea on the *Titanic*, supervised by Mr. Gatti, would have been on par with the hotel's standards.

I have been the tour guide on many "tea-tours" to England. The majority of the travelers were taking their first trip to England, and after several days in London, the groups are escorted into the library of a 17th century, elegant manor house. The village of Lower Slaughter in the heart of the Cotswolds, considered by many to be one of the most lovely locations in all of England, was the setting for our wonderful afternoon tea. The experience was in every aspect equivalent to afternoon tea at *Downton Abbey*. The food was divine and the service fastidious. Our every wish for the perfect afternoon tea was provided. From the starched white linen napkins to the exquisite petits fours, the tea was magnificent.

The time we ladies spent together was the real essence of experiencing the pleasure of tea. One of my guests on the "tea-tour" brought her 80 year-old mother. They were having a great time and the mother told me, "This is more than tea, it is a lifetime memory."

Afternoon tea, such as the one we experienced in the Cotswolds, provides an intimate setting for the hostess and her guests. In *Downton Abbey*, Violet, the Dowager Countess of Grantham, entertains many guests in this dramatic series. Her table in the drawing room was beautifully arranged and covered with a Battenberg lace tablecloth upon which sat beautiful china teacups and saucers, and an assortment of tea sandwiches, scones and pastries. A silver tipping teapot was used to pour each guest a cup of tea.

Yes, tea time is a most civilized meal. When we make time, setting aside the urgent, and create a space for those little extras that feed our soul and nurture our senses, that is when it happens...the pleasures of teatime. It is a celebration of friendship, offering comfort to those in your personal circle.

There is something about tea that brings out the very essence of hospitality. The pleasures of tea are many things to many people, and I am delighted that I get to be a part of that story. I love the following quotation by a French writer, "The reconstitution of the past is a delicate pleasure of which one should not be deprived." I agree.

"There are few hours in my life more agreeable than the hour
dedicated to the ceremony known as afternoon tea."

- HENRY JAMES

CHAPTER 8

Downton Abbey Tea

• • •

An Elegant Tea

EVERYTIME WE HAVE TEA, WE celebrate. It could be a birthday, a wedding, a homecoming, a new baby, or friendship, but it is a celebration. Tea, without question, is one of the most sociable events of the day. The British have exalted the afternoon tea event to a lovely pastime that is now being revived all over the world. After all, Queen Elizabeth fell in love with Prince Phillip at a wedding tea in 1934.

Downton Abbey has played an enormous role in elevating this sublime mealtime to an even higher level. With more than 200 million viewers worldwide, *Downton Abbey* is being watched in over 200 countries. Just as the blockbuster, *Titanic*, more than 500 million people have viewed the movie since it was released in 1997. The Edwardian era has been revived. In that time period, afternoon tea was the norm. Not only the very wealthy entertained at home, but the middle classes were emerging and began opening their homes to friends and family. Welcoming others to our homes has always been an expression of hospitality. I invite you, teacup in hand, to begin the planning for your own *Downton Abbey* Tea.

Plan – Plan - Plan

Women of the early 1900s didn't have the luxury of the many conveniences we have today. Meals were made from scratch, not mixes; refrigeration was not in every home; and electrical appliances were in short supply. Most women I know do not want to go back to that era, but we do like the elegance and grandeur of that time. Women love beautiful things, the crisp linens covering the table, the gleaming silver tea service, and the special touches of flowers and music. While those "upstairs" at *Downton Abbey* had the privilege of being served, we will be the ones providing the service for our friends. The "pleasure of your company" is going to be our theme for this wonderful British event.

"What with these toasters and mixers and such like, we'd be out of a job."

MRS. PATMORE

Afternoon Tea Check List

Having the assistance of Mr. Carson, the head butler who runs the household of *Downton Abbey*, with the cooperation of Mrs. Hughes, the head housekeeper, the planning for this afternoon tea would be easy.

Everything would have been prepared without a hitch. The table would be set properly with Mr. Carson having chosen the china and flatwear, and double-checking that each plate is in the correct place. When all the guests are seated, he will also oversee the serving of the food, in proper order, and never would a teacup be empty.

Two Weeks Before:

- Set the date and time
- Decide on a theme – *Downton Abbey*
- Determine guest list
- Make or buy invitations
- Mail invitations
- Plan a menu
- Determine a budget

One Week Before:

- Check table linens and napkins
- Shop for food items
- Prepare any menu items that can be made ahead and frozen
- Buy or make party favors
- Wash serving pieces, glassware and silverware
- Polish silver if necessary
- Follow up with guests who have not RSVP'd
- Create place cards

Two Days Before:

- Buy additional food items
- Write place cards and determine seating arrangement
- Pick up and arrange flowers
- Plan any music you wish to play

The Day Before:

- Prepare sandwich fillings
- Bake scones
- Prepare desserts
- Set table and arrange place cards and favors

Morning of:

- Finish preparing all food
- Check guest bathroom, set out clean towels
- Bake scones if not done day before
- Have kitchen clean with new trash bag and dishwasher empty

Two hours before:

- Put your feet up and have a cup of tea

One hour before:

- Get dressed
- Fill tea kettles with fresh water
- Place scones on cookie sheet and cover with foil
- Enjoy!

Invitations

How many people to invite? Usually tea parties will be kept to eight people or fewer. If you desire to have a larger event, have several tables set up to mix those old friends with new acquaintances. The tea party should be a relaxed event so that everyone attending will enjoy such a special time together. The amount of china and silver you have is also a critical factor when deciding whom to invite. Other considerations are the size of your room, your time-frame for the set-up, and cooking schedule. It is a wonderful idea to invite a friend to help you with the menu and the preparation of the food.

What says *Downton Abbey* more than elegant invitations? This is the tea that needs a formal and elaborate invitation to set the stage. An invitation lets your guests know what to wear, what time to come and where the event will be held. A Victorian afternoon tea demands the best. The invitations can be hand-written, engraved, or done in calligraphy on beautiful parchment stationery, a beautiful flowery note card, or plain white card stock. The look should be bold and romantic. Black and white with a touch of color will set the tone for a unique and unforgettable celebration. If you desire to embellish the invitation, a small ribbon, silk or dried flowers, will give your invitation a vintage look.

Now that you have chosen the perfect invitation for your tea, here are the details to be included:

Name of hostess
Theme of tea
Date
Time
Location
Dress code
RSVP and last date to respond.

For a formal tea such as this, it is important to set the date and stick to it. Nothing is worse than changing the date because someone can't come. It is your party-choose the best date for you. The invitations should be sent out at least two weeks in advance and the date to respond should be no fewer than three days before your tea. Any more days and you will find it difficult to prepare.

Write the day, month, and date, to avoid confusion. Also include a phone number or an email to send their response. If necessary, include a map with the invitation for ease of the guests arriving at your home.

Example:

Mrs. Joan Smith would like to extend an invitation to attend a
Downton Abbey Tea
Saturday, August 29, 2014
at
Three o'clock in the afternoon
Hosted at her home
Two twenty two Lakeview Drive,
Denver, Colorado
Please wear your *Downton Abbey* inspired clothing
Hats and gloves suggested.
RSVP – 222-222-2222 or an email address
Please respond by Wednesday, August 26th at the latest

The Tea Table

The traditional *Downton Abbey* tea table will have a white tablecloth, bone china tea set and some glistening pieces of silver. The tradition of an afternoon tea has always linked its history to that of charm and elegance. Nowhere is that more obvious than in the lovely patterns of chintz or floral-appointed bone china. Whether you have matched china sets, or you are blending teacups and plates from several patterns, plan ahead before setting the table. Color unifies the table and compliments the food served.

The table is comparable to a stage. All the accouterments are the players. The outcome begins with the backdrop. Since most china has a pattern, solid-colored tablecloths are the best choice. The color of the napkins and flowers should be coordinated with your china and the tablecloth to give the table a sophisticated and uniform look. Lace was very popular in the 1900s, so you could use that as an overlay on the table.

An attractive table setting is only one part of the atmosphere you are creating, but it can be the most captivating part of the whole scene. Collecting bone china teacups has been a passion most of my life. Looking at all the teacups I have collected over the many years brings me much pleasure and comfort. A tea table with an eclectic array of cups is more interesting than a matching set, and always a conversation-starter.

Set the table the night before your tea. Get creative and be original. It's nice to have varied heights in your serving pieces. Many stores now carry cake plate holders as regular stock. There is no right or wrong way to combine china. If you are using your china place settings, layer the plates for a more elegant look. If you are just starting out, use the best you have for this kind of event. Then add to it as time and money permits. A teapot should be one of the first items to acquire. Then begin to buy teacups, plates, and silver pieces (however, you might find a great buy on a few teacups, or a silver tea strainer, so go for it!) Something that many women do if they do not have enough teacups is have each guest bring her favorite teacup and then tell why it is special to her.

I have now collected plates to go with most of my teacups. I love to find a trio set, which is the matching teacup, saucer, and tea plate. Before I had these, I would use a plate that didn't match, and place a paper doily on the plate and cover it with a clear glass plate from the dollar store. This has worked for many women as they continue to collect. If you have a china dinner set, then use it, as it sets a beautiful table. When placing the dishes on your table, allow 24 inches for each guest's setting.

Place Cards

Place cards are one of the little details that make teatime so charming. Tent-style cards are easy to find in most stationery departments. To keep the elegant look of Downton Abbey, write the guest's name in calligraphy. If you are assigning one of the characters to your guests, have that name on the place card. Dainty porcelain place cards are also another fun purchase, as they are reusable and can double as markers for foods in buffet settings. Place cards are for the hostess's benefit as much as the guests. The guest knows where to sit, and is placed next to someone with whom they might have common interests. For instance, a quiet person seated next to someone more outgoing will foster conversation.

Silver Accouterments

Silverware, silver trays and silver teapots should be polished and gleaming to have center stage on your tea table. If you have any silver, this is the time to bring it out. Silver cake stands and teapots always seem to be in a tea setting on *Downton Abbey*. I love the charm and elegance that silver adds to the table setting. Silver was prevalent during the Victorian and Edwardian eras, but with the invention of silver-plate and stainless steel, silver polishing seems to have become a dreaded chore. This has resulted in silver tea accouterments becoming collectors' items.

Many antique stores and flea markets are excellent places to find silver pieces for your tea collection. Look for tea strainers in all shapes and sizes, serving spoons, dessert forks, moat spoons, teaspoons, sugar tongs, trays, teapots, creamers and sugar bowls.

~ Menu ~

A formal afternoon tea will have three courses and served in this order:
Sandwiches
Scones
Sweets

(A glass of sparkling elderflower wine or champagne may be served before the sandwiches)

Tea Sandwiches

Roast beef and horseradish
Egg mayonnaise
Triple-Decker Cucumber
Smoked salmon
Chelsea Curry Chicken

Scones

Classic Lemon Scones
Norfolk Lavender Scones

Sweets

Madeleines
Fruit Tarts
Victoria Sponge Cake with Madeira Cream

Teas

English Breakfast
Earl Grey

Recipes for a Downton Abbey Tea

1ˢᵀ Course ~ Sandwiches

Roast beef and horseradish

3 Tablespoons mayonnaise
2 teaspoons prepared horseradish
10 thin slices white sandwich bread
1/3 lb. lean roast beef, sliced thin
Salt and freshly ground pepper, to taste
Butter, room temperature

In a small bowl, stir together the mayonnaise and horseradish. Spread the bread slices first with a thin layer of butter, then with the mayonnaise mixture. Layer the roast beef on 5 slices of the bread and season with salt and pepper. Top each with one of the remaining bread slices.

Using a sharp or electric knife, trim the crusts off the sandwiches. Cut the sandwiches diagonally into quarters and arrange on a serving platter. Makes 20 tea sandwiches.

Egg Mayonnaise

6 hard boiled eggs, peeled, then soaked in Earl Grey tea for several hours, then, finely chopped.
1/4 cup fine chopped green onion
1/4 cup sweet pickle relish or Branston Pickle (chopped fine)
1/3 cup mayonnaise
1/2 teaspoon salt
1/4 teaspoon pepper
Thin white bread

Combine all ingredients well, chill, then spread thinly on buttered slices of bread. Trim crusts and cut into desired shapes. Serves 8

Triple-Decker Cucumber

*This triple- decker sandwich adds variety and interest to your tea table.
The mint and onion give the cucumbers a refreshing taste.*

12 slices of white sandwich bread
1 English cucumber, washed and sliced into ¼ inch rounds, then drained onto paper towels.
8 ounces of cream cheese, softened
1/3 cup of fresh mint, finely chopped
1/3 cup green onion, finely chopped
Salt and pepper to taste

Combine the cream cheese, mint and onion. Add salt and pepper
Spread the cream cheese mixture on one side of each slice of bread.
Layer the cucumber slices on 4 slices of bread, then top with a slice of bread that has both sides spread with cream cheese.
Layer more cucumber slices on top of second slice of bread, then top with the last slice of bread, cream cheese side down.
Using an electric knife, trim away the crusts and cut each triple-decker sandwich into triangles. Be careful not to push down hard on the top slice of bread. Makes 12 tea sandwiches.

Smoked Salmon

4 Tablespoons softened butter
1 Tablespoon fresh dill, chopped
Squeeze of lemon juice
8 pieces of smoked salmon
¼ English cucumber, grated
10 slices of firm, thin, brown bread
Sea salt and freshly ground pepper

Mix together the butter, dill, lemon juice, cucumber, and salt and pepper.
Spread the butter mixture onto the bread slices.
Place a slice of salmon onto each buttered bread slice.
Top with the remaining slices of bread.
Trim crusts from bread and slice each sandwich into 4 triangles.
Makes 16 tea sandwiches

Chelsea Curry Chicken

The House of Commons Tea Room in Denver, Colorado, is a wonderful place to have afternoon tea. I have been many times and each time I am there, I almost think I am in England. I have grown to love the owner, Jessica, who welcomes each and every guest into her tea room, as though it were her own home. This wonderful chicken salad makes a delicious tea sandwich, but is equally as good served on a bed of lettuce.

3 large boneless, skinless, chicken breasts
2 teaspoons medium curry powder
½ cup mayonnaise
½ cup plain yogurt
½ cup diced celery
1/3 cup raisins

Rub chicken breasts with olive oil and sprinkle with salt and pepper.
Cover chicken breasts with parchment paper that has been rubbed with olive oil on side next to chicken.
Roast in 400° F oven for 35 minutes.

Chop chicken into small cubes.
Mix mayonnaise and yogurt together.
Add celery, curry powder and raisins.
Combine all ingredients with chicken.

Spread softened butter onto 12 slices of wheat bread.
Evenly spread chicken salad onto 6 slices of bread, top each with buttered bread slices.
Trim crusts and cut each sandwich into three strips.
Keep covered with damp paper towels until ready to serve.

Serves 36 tea sandwiches

2ᴺᴰ Course ~ Scones

Lemon Classic Scones

3 cups self-raising flour, plus some for dusting
¼ teaspoon salt
1 teaspoon baking powder
1/3 cup unsalted butter, cut into cubes
3 Tablespoons sugar
½ cup whole milk
1 teaspoon vanilla extract
½ lemon, squeezed
1 beaten egg for glaze

Preheat oven to 425° F

Place flour into a large bowl; add salt and baking powder and mix.
Add the butter and use a pastry blender until the mix looks like fine crumbs. Stir in the sugar.
Heat the milk in the microwave for about 30 seconds until warm.
Add the vanilla and lemon juice to the milk, set aside for a minute.
Make a well in the dry mix, then add the milk mixture and combine it quickly with a knife.
Sprinkle some flour onto a counter and place the dough on the flour.
Knead the dough several times until it is a little smooth.
Pat into a round about 2 inches deep.

Use a cookie or biscuit cutter that has been dipped into some flour.
Cut dough and place it onto a cookie sheet.
Press out remaining dough to make additional scones.
Brush tops with beaten egg.
Bake for 10 minutes until golden on top.
Serve warm with jam and Devonshire cream.

Norfolk Lavender Scones

My grandparents owned a cottage near the Norfolk Lavender Farm on the West Coast of England. The lovely fragrance from the nearly 100 acres of lavender, added a special experience to the beautiful countryside and glorious coastline. Freshly picked lavender or the use of culinary lavender gives these scones a lovely scent and are delicious served warm with clotted cream. Since lavender is a herb, it can be added to a traditional black tea for a delightful treat. Use lavender sparingly, as its flavor is quite strong. I don't use jam on this scone, as it is already so flavorful.

    2 cups of self-raising flour
    1 teaspoon baking powder
    ¼ cup unsalted butter, cut into cubes
    1/3 cup lavender sugar*
    2/3 cup buttermilk
    ½ teaspoon salt

Preheat oven to 425° F
Line cookie sheet with parchment paper
Mix flour and baking powder together, then add butter and blend into flour with pastry blender or two knives.
Add the sugar and mix well.
Stir in the buttermilk and only add enough to create a soft dough.
Place dough onto floured surface and knead a few times. Do not over-knead, as this makes the scones tough.
Pat into a round about ¾ inch thick.
Cut into 8 triangles and place on baking sheet with about 1 inch between the scones.
Brush the tops with buttermilk.
Bake for 10 to 12 minutes until golden brown.
Serve warm

*To make lavender sugar: Mix two Tablespoons of lavender into 1/3 cup of sugar. Place into a covered jar and let sit for at least 24 hours.

Clotted Cream or Devonshire Cream

Nothing tastes better than real clotted cream from England. Clotted cream can come from Devon, Cornwall, or Somerset counties, as the breed of cattle have a high content of cream in their milk. In the United States, jars of clotted cream or Devon cream are sold at gourmet and import markets. It's good, but not like the real thing.

This recipe is a good substitute and should be made using heavy whipping cream. The more fat content a cream contains, the more stable the cream will be in a whipped state. Heavy whipping cream has about 38% fat, while whipping cream has 30% to 33% fat. In previous recipes, I have added sugar and sour cream, but in reality, clotted cream is just cream. The yellow food coloring gives it an authentic color. Make sure the cream is very cold. Chill the beaters and bowl in the freezer for 15 minutes before beating.

8 ounces heavy whipping cream
1 Tablespoon cream cheese
Yellow food coloring – just a few drops to give a light, buttery look.

Whip the cream on low in a large bowl to prevent splattering. Beat for 30 seconds until bubbles begin to form on the top, add food coloring, then increase the mixer speed to medium or high and beat until the cream begins to thicken. Slowly add the cream cheese and continue beating until stiff peaks form. Don't forget to use a spatula to include the cream on the bottom and sides of the bowl. Store in a glass container with a tight fitting lid.
Makes 2 cups of clotted cream.

There is a long-running rivalry between Devon and Cornwall and the proper order of placing the cream on a scone. The folks in Cornwall believe the jam goes on the scone first, then the cream on top. Those in Devon insist that the cream should be placed on the scone first, then the jam on top! I have always put the cream on first and top it with the jam…it spreads easier, but the most important thing to do is cut your scone in half, put the jam and cream on each half, and <u>never</u> put them back together! Or eat with a fork!

3RD COURSE ~ SWEETS

Madeleines

These sweet little French cakes are often thought of as cookies. They are the perfect accompaniment to this delightful Downton Abbey Tea. I recommend having two madeleine pans as this recipe makes 24 little spongy cakes. It is much easier to bake them together rather than have to wash and rebutter the pans between baking. Watch the butter carefully as you melt it; only brown just a little, as the butter can go from light to burnt very quickly. Ask your friends if they have a madeleine pan you can borrow, so you will only need to buy one.

1 stick of unsalted butter
1 cup flour
2/3 cup sugar
2 large eggs
¾ teaspoon vanilla extract
1 teaspoon salt
1 Tablespoon lemon juice
1 Tablespoon lemon zest
Powdered sugar for sifting on top

Melt the butter and brown very slightly.
Pour into a small bowl immediately to stop the browning process.
Using a whisk, mix the flour and sugar.
Mix the eggs, vanilla, salt, lemon juice, and lemon zest with electric mixer until the mixture is thick and pale yellow.
Add the egg mixture to the flour, using a spatula and gently stir until just combined.
Add the butter and combine with mixer until it is well blended in to the mixture.
Cover the batter with plastic wrap and refrigerate for at least two hours.

Prepare the Madeleine pans by spraying very well with baking spray, or melted butter spread into the molds with a pastry brush and then dusted with flour.

Place the pans into freezer for 15 minutes.

Preheat the oven to 350° F

Remove pans from freezer and fill each well in the pans with a generous Tablespoon of batter.

Do not smooth out the batter, but leave it mounded as this is what gives the domed appearance to the Madeleines.

Place both pans into the oven and bake for 8 to 10 minutes.

The edges should be golden brown and the centers should spring back after pushing slightly in the center with your finger.

Do not overbake.

Remove the pans from the oven and tap them against the counter to release.

Let them cool for just a couple minutes, then gently remove from pan and place on cooling rack.

If needed, use a fork and gently loosen the madeleines from the molds.

When cool, sprinkle lightly with powdered sugar and serve.

Store in an airtight container.

Best served in a couple days or freeze.

Dust with powdered sugar before serving.

Makes 24

Fruit Tarts

Tarts are one of the main-stays of Victorian and Edwardian teas. Whether on land or sea, a fruit tart will always be a welcome addition to an elegant tea. If you use a premade pie crust or make your own, the filling will be the crowing touch to heavenly conclusion for your Downton Abbey *tea.*

Pastry Shell:

    1 stick of butter, melted
    ½ cup sugar
    ½ teaspoon vanilla
    ½ teaspoon salt
    1 ½ cup flour

Filling:

    ½ cup heavy whipping cream
    ½ cup lemon curd -*microwave lemon curd recipe
    2 cups of berries – a combination of strawberries, blueberries, raspberries, or blackberries.
    1 Tablespoon of orange liqueur
    1 Tablespoon sugar

Butter 8 small tart pans

In a large bowl, mix butter and sugar until well blended.
Add vanilla, salt, and flour, and mix to form a soft dough.
Divide the dough into eight pieces and place each piece in the center of the buttered tart pans.
Press the dough out on the bottom and sides of the tart pans.

Preheat oven to 350° F

Poke holes with fork tines into the bottom of the dough so it doesn't puff up while baking.

Bake until the dough is golden brown, usually about 15 minutes.

Remove from oven and cool.

Beat the cream until thick peaks form.

Fold the lemon curd into the cream gently until combined.

Cut up berries into quarters or until all are uniformly the same size.

Add liqueur and sugar to the fruit and stir.

Let this mixture sit for about 15 minutes.

Spoon the lemon cream into the cooled tart shells, then top with the berry mixture.

Top the tarts with a few small, fresh mint leaves.

Keep refrigerated until ready to serve.

Microwave Lemon Curd

I have used this recipe for years. With the price of a jar of lemon curd, this is a great alternative.
(From - *365 Quick and Easy Microwave Recipes*)

½ stick of butter
½ cup sugar
1/3 cup freshly squeezed lemon juice
1 ½ teaspoons freshly grated lemon zest
3 eggs, beaten.

In a 4 cup glass measuring container, place the butter, sugar, lemon juice and lemon zest, and stir to blend.
Cook on high in microwave for 4 minutes, then stir.
Slowly whisk in a small amount of the hot butter mixture into the beaten eggs, then whisk the egg mixture back into the butter mixture and cook on high for 1 ½ to 2 minutes.
Whisk until smooth, then cook for another minute or two, until thickened. Whisk again until smooth. Pour into glass jars and seal. Refrigerate and use up within a month.

Victoria Sponge Cake with Madeira Cream

This cake has been served to Queens and Kings. Several scenes in Downton Abbey *show this cake at tea time. It's a perfect addition to your very elegant* Downton Abbey *tea. The cake is light, buttery, and fluffy. The filling is exquisite. Serve on a footed cake plate and surround the cake with edible flowers, such as day lily, nasturtiums, begonias, carnations, lilac, or pansies. Make sure that no pesticides or other chemicals have been applied to these flowers.*

Cake:

> 1 cup butter, room temperature
> 1 cup sugar (most recipes call for caster sugar as granulated sugar is rather coarse) To make caster sugar place granulated sugar in a food processor.
> 4 eggs, room temperature-beaten
> 2 cups self-rising flour, sifted

Cream butter and sugar until light and fluffy.
Add eggs and mix well.
Grease two 8 inch round cake tins with butter, and line with parchment paper,
Divide batter between the two pans and smooth tops to make even.
Bake 20 to 25 minutes.
Cool 10 to 15 minutes in pans, then turn out onto wire racks to continue cooling.

Filling:

> 1 container of heavy whipping cream
> ¼ cup sugar
> ¼ cup Madeira Wine

Combine the sugar and wine and mix until completely blended.
Slowly add in the whipping cream, then beat with electric mixer until stiff peaks form, about 10 minutes.
Place one cake layer bottom side up on cake plate.
Spread the cream over the cake layer.
Place 2nd layer bottom side down on top of the cream.
Dust the top of the cake with sifted powdered sugar.
Refrigerate cake until ready to serve.
Decorate with flowers or fresh fruit.

"Tea, though ridiculed by those who are naturally coarse in their nervous sensibilities, will always be the favorite beverage of the intellectual."

- Thomas de Quincey

CHAPTER 9

Celebrating Birthdays

• • •

Downton Abbey Style

Don't count your years, make your years count.

EVERYONE, EVERY YEAR, HAS A birthday. What an elegant party we could have at *Downton Abbey*. I would love Lady Mary to be in charge, plan the menu and guest list, dress for the occasion, and be our hostess. However, since most of us won't be invited to have our special day in the castle, let's bring *Downton Abbey* to our homes! The results can be delightful, not only for the birthday girl, but also for the guests.

Some women don't like to celebrate their birthdays with a lot of fuss, however, I'm not one of them. I love to join others in a celebration. Birthdays are good for us, the more we have, the longer we live.

Every year on your birthday, you get the chance to start over.

When I was a child, my birthdays were always very special. This might be the reason I still love to celebrate on my special day. On my birthday I didn't have to make my bed. That was unusual, as every other day of the year it was mandatory. I also chose the menu for the entire day. My birthday party was planned weeks in advance and, being the only girl in the family, it was special. Most of the parties were planned around a tea theme, even the one where a pony showed up to give all the children rides.

My day began with a special breakfast. No bacon and eggs for me, I wanted fruit and crumpets. Since it was difficult to buy crumpets, my mother usually made them. The grand finale was dinner. As soon as my father walked into the house from work, the party began. Balloons and streamers filled the hallway and dining room. Then came the presents, followed by my favorite cake, coconut. Those days were special.

In season four, Lord Grantham celebrates his birthday at *Downton Abbey* with a very posh dinner surrounded by family and friends. No one ages in this series, even though it transports us from 1912 to 1924. Might it be that Julian Fellows, the creator, producer, and sole writer of the scripts, wants to keep our attention from the changing years?

Birthdays were celebrated in the Edwardian times with some amusing traditions. One especially enduring ritual was the baking of coins and trinkets into the birthday cake. Whoever found the coin was predicted to become rich in later life; but the one who found a thimble in the slice of cake might never marry. Games and gifts were also part of the celebration.

Women love afternoon teas, so including the celebration of a birthday is a great reason to plan an afternoon tea party. I have initiated many birthday teas for friends and family, but I have also been invited to teas that the birthday girl herself designed. I don't think it matters who does what - the main purpose is to celebrate!

Birthdays are meant to be spent with family and friends. A birthday is the one day that we are the oldest we will ever be, and the youngest we will ever be again. Like the old saying "age only matters if you are cheese or wine," we ladies think that letting others know our age is still a private matter. Does a party make you turn older? The age of the person has nothing to do with a birthday party and it's a silly reason not to observe a special day. Maybe we need to look at birthdays as an advantage. We shouldn't regret growing older – it's a privilege denied to many.

Recently, I celebrated the 147th birthday of Margaret Brown at the Molly Brown House in Denver. (A birthday in her honor.) I met her great-granddaughter, Helen, and after the birthday party we arranged to meet for tea. My book, *Tea on the Titanic*, included a chapter about her great-grandmother. She was thrilled to know I had researched the history books about Margaret and included her in my book. That connection cemented our bond, and over the past several years we have become great friends. We have spoken together at various events, and were privileged to be guests at the opening night celebrations of the new musical, *The Unsinkable Molly Brown*. Our relationship has been a delight, and to think it all started at a birthday party. I am thankful for Helen's link to history that she so unselfishly shares.

I have included a *Molly Brown Tea* in this book, as it brings together all the components needed for a beautiful event. Since Mrs. Brown was of the same time period as *Downton Abbey*, I am sure she could have been included in many of their social affairs. Maybe she was a dear friend of Martha Levinson, the American mother of Cora Crawley, Lady Grantham. The cash-poor affairs of many manor homes in England during the late 1800s required land-rich owners to marry American heiresses in order to secure the financial future of their inheritance. Cora Crawley brought a very large fortune to *Downton Abbey*, which proved useful for the estate to remain in the Crawley family.

Preparing an afternoon tea is an opportunity to share and maybe even restore friendships. Many years ago, I offended a co-worker and couldn't seem to make amends. I began to pray for a solution, and the answer to my prayer seemed to be: "Plan a birthday tea party for her." So, I bit the bullet and made the suggestion. I was delighted that she eagerly accepted my offer. Her guest list included a few nurses from work, but were mainly her close friends. We set the date, and planned an afternoon tea in her honor. Every invitee attended, and the afternoon was remarkable. It was my way of offering my apology in a tangible way, and my co-worker offered me forgiveness.

Taking a tea party to your friend's home is another way of enjoying the gift of tea. Place your tea items in a basket and transform her living room into an English tearoom. If that is not feasible, then celebrate her birthday at your home. If we wait to share acts of kindness when the situation is just right, we might miss some great opportunities to bless others. It's those everyday, common occasions when we can transform the ordinary into something grand. A *Downton Abbey* inspired tea can bring great joy to the birthday girl. Prepare everything you can ahead of time, except for the tea. Then we can sit and sip with others. Wouldn't it be lovely for Mrs. Patmore and Daisy to show up now, and help us plan the perfect *Downton Abbey* Birthday tea?

A birthday is just the first day of another 365-day trip around the sun.

Is a birthday an excuse to have a party? YES!

Let's get started:

   Plan a date
   Set a theme
   Make a Guest List
   Send Invitations
   Select Music
   Plan decorations
   Plan Menu
   Plan Entertainment – Games? Favors?

Birthday Tea Menu

Tea Sandwiches

Tomato Tartlets
Cranberry, Turkey, and Arugula Sandwiches
Curried Egg Tea Sandwiches
Open-face Cucumber Sandwiches

Scones

Cinnamon Circle Scones
Cranberry Scones with Buttermilk Glaze

Sweets or Desserts

White Chocolate Dipped Strawberries
No-bake Chocolate Truffles
Cherished Coconut Wine Cake

Tea

Mango Black Tea
English Black Tea
Darjeeling

Recipes

Tea Sandwiches and Savories

Tomato Tartlets

3 packages mini phyllo tart shells
1 small can Ro-Tel tomatoes, well drained
1 cup mayonnaise
1/3 cup bacon bits
1/3 cup shredded Swiss cheese

Preheat oven to 350° F

Combine tomatoes, mayonnaise, bacon bits and cheese.
Fill the shells with the tomato mixture.
Bake for 10 to 15 minutes.

Makes 45 tartlets

Cranberry, Turkey, and Arugula Sandwiches

I first tasted arugula in England. It was called rocket lettuce and I had a terrible time finding it in our American super markets. The taste is very unique, and like most leafy greens, it is high in Vitamin A, C, K, and folate, and is a great source of calcium and magnesium. Its peppery taste is a great addition to salads, pastas, and sandwiches.

Butter, softened
White or whole wheat bread, 20 slices
Turkey, 1/3 pound thinly sliced
1 bunch arugula
1 can (14 ounce) cranberry jelly

Butter one side of each bread surface.
Spread a thin layer of cranberry jelly on top of the butter.
On half the bread slices, lay a slice of turkey and a layer of arugula on top of the jelly
Place the other slices on top of the lettuce, and press lightly to seal.
Trim the crusts with an electric knife, and cut into triangles.
Place into air-tight containers, top with damp paper towels, and seal until ready to serve.
Makes 40 quarter tea sandwiches.

Curried Egg Tea Sandwiches

There is an age-old debate on the best way to boil eggs so that peeling is easy. I have tried many different ways; sometimes the eggs peel effortlessly with the egg white intact, and other times it is a mess. This way works most of the time, but I believe the age of the egg is the key; fresher eggs peel easier. Check eggs in the grocery store before buying them for the date on the end of the carton, and don't be fooled by all the hype of being organic, range free, etc. The best eggs are those bought from a local farmer you trust.

6 large eggs, room temperature
2 finely chopped green onions
1 teaspoon curry
½ teaspoon Dijon mustard
1/3 cup mayonnaise
Salt and white pepper to taste

20 slices of thin white bread, frozen
Room temperature butter

Place the eggs in a large saucepan of cold water and bring to a boil.
Cover, remove from heat, and let stand for 15 minutes.
Drain the eggs and fill pan with cold water. Replace the water to keep it cold.
After 15 minutes, peel the eggs and pat dry.
Finely mash the eggs and add the mayonnaise, curry, mustard, salt and pepper.
Butter the bread slices and top 10 slices with the egg salad mixture.
Trim the crusts and cut into squares.
Keep covered with damp paper towels and sealed in airtight container until ready to serve.
Makes 40 quarter sandwiches

Open-Face Cucumber Sandwiches

1 English hot house cucumber
12 slices pumpernickel or 1 package Pepperidge Farm Pumpernickel Party Bread
8 ounces softened cream cheese
¼ cup mayonnaise
¼ teaspoon garlic powder
¼ teaspoon salt
1 Tablespoon dill
Parsley leaves or fresh dill leaves

Strip the sides of the cucumber with a fork.
Slice the cucumber into thin round slices
Place cucumber slices on sheets of paper towel to drain.
Cut the bread into circles about the size of the cucumber slices.
Cream together the cheese and mayonnaise, add the spices.
Spread one side of the bread rounds with the cheese mixture.
Top with a slice of cucumber.
Decorate the top of the slice with a squirt of cream cheese mixture and top with parsley leaf or fresh dill sprig.

Makes 24 tea sandwiches

SCONES

Cinnamon Circle Scones

On a recent trip to England, we were served these scones in a tearoom in Bath. This recipe is from the book, Bath's Tea Time Treats.

Preheat oven to 400° F.

2 ¼ cups self-rising flour
¼ cup butter
¼ cup sugar
½ cup milk
¼ cup melted butter
1 teaspoon cinnamon

Combine butter and flour with a pastry blender until it resembles coarse crumbs.
Stir in the sugar until well mixed.
Add the milk and stir until you have a soft dough.
Roll out the dough on a flour-lined surface into a rectangle about 6" x 12".
Brush the melted butter onto the dough and then sprinkle with cinnamon.
Roll the dough up like a jelly roll, starting at the short end.
Cut into ½ inch slices.
Place on a parchment lined cookie sheet.
Bake until golden brown, about 8 to 10 minutes.
Cool on a baking rack.
Serve with clotted cream and jam if desired.

Makes 12 scones.

Cranberry Scones with Buttermilk Glaze

I conducted a workshop last year to educate and encourage women from my church to host afternoon teas in their home. Many of the women had never given a tea, so we had a lot of fun trying new recipes and eating our endeavors. One of the attendees was new to our women's group, but not new to giving teas. Terri and her twin sister Sherri traveled to a very elegant Bed and Breakfast in Kentucky every winter, prepared all the food, and served the inn's annual Christmas tea. We were delighted to have her expertise, and this lovely scone recipe.

   3 cups all-purpose flour
   1/3 cup sugar
   2 ½ teaspoons baking powder
   ½ teaspoon baking soda
   ½ teaspoon salt
   ¾ cup butter
   1 cup buttermilk
   ¾ cup dried cranberries

Glaze

   1 Tablespoon heavy whipping cream
   ½ teaspoon cinnamon
   2 Tablespoons sugar

Preheat oven to 425° F.
Do not grease cookie sheet

Combine flour, sugar, baking powder, baking soda and salt in a large mixing bowl.
Use a whisk or fork to mix well.
Cut the butter into the flour mixture using a pastry blender until the mixture looks like coarse breadcrumbs.

Add the buttermilk and the dried cranberries, mix until the dry ingredients are mixed.

Shape the dough into a ball and press it together until it holds together.

Place the ball onto a lightly floured surface and knead about 10 to 12 times, then pat into a circle about ½ inch thick.

Mix the glaze ingredients together and blend.

Brush the mixture on top of the dough.

Cut the dough circle into 16 to 18 pie shaped pieces, or scones

Place the scones one inch apart on the baking sheet.

Bake for 12 to 14 minutes until the tops are browned.

Serve with jam and clotted cream.

Makes 16 to 18 scones.

SWEETS

"You can be gorgeous at thirty, charming at forty, and irresistible for the rest of your life."
Coco Chanel

White Chocolate Dipped Strawberries

12 large strawberries with stem (or one for each guest)
1 cup chopped nuts
1 ½ cups white chocolate chips

Rinse strawberries with very cold water, then blot and dry well with paper towels.

Melt the chocolate in a deep microwave-safe bowl, stirring occasionally until melted and smooth.

Line a cookie sheet with wax paper.

Dip the strawberries into the melted chocolate, then sprinkle the chopped nuts over the strawberries.

Refrigerate the berries for at least several hours.

Remove and place on a serving dish.

No-bake Chocolate Truffles

No birthday party should be without chocolate. My granddaughter Nicole has tested many of the recipes in this book. This was one of her favorites that we shared via email.

1/3 cup butter, softened
1/3 cup brown sugar
2 teaspoons vanilla
1 cup flour
1 cup chocolate chips (milk chocolate, white chocolate, or butterscotch)
¾ cup semi-sweet chocolate chips to dip truffle into.
Garnishes if desired: chopped nuts, pretzels, or sea salt.

Mix together butter, sugar and vanilla.
Add flour ½ cup at a time and mix until it is just combined with the butter mixture.
Stir in the chocolate chips and roll into one-inch balls.
Place on a wax-paper lined cookie sheet.
Place in freezer for 20 to 30 minutes.
After the dough has become firm, melt the semi-sweet chocolate chips in the microwave. Dip the cookie dough balls into the chocolate with a fork or skewer and tap off the excess chocolate. Put the chocolate balls back onto the wax paper and sprinkle with one of the garnishes. Place back into the freezer until the chocolate is hard. Store in covered container in the refrigerator.

You can never have too many candles on your birthday cake.

Cherished Coconut Wine Cake

In the late 1990s I entered a contest and won a luncheon date with Nancy Lindemeyer, the founding editor of Victoria Magazine. Lunch was served in a private dining room at the Bel-Air Hotel, in Beverly Hills, California. I loved Victoria Magazine and had been an avid reader for many years, and in fact I still have most of the copies from the years she was editor (1987 to 2000). Whenever I bake this cake it reminds me of that wonderful luncheon with a very classy lady. This recipe appeared in the June 1997 issue of Victoria Magazine. Victoria Magazine ceased publications in 2003 and is now being republished by Hoffman Media, which also publishes Tea Time magazine and Southern Lady. A recent issue featured Highclere Castle, the pictoral setting for Downton Abbey.

2 ½ cups flour
2 ¼ teaspoons baking powder
½ teaspoon salt
2 cups sugar
4 large eggs
1 cup of vegetable oil
1 cup dry white wine
1 teaspoon vanilla

To make the frosting:
2 ¼ cups sour cream
2 Tablespoons heavy cream
1 teaspoon vanilla
6 cups shredded coconut
1 cup sifted powdered sugar

Preheat oven to 350° F

Sift together the flour, baking powder and salt.

With an electric mixer, beat sugar with the eggs until well mixed.

Add the oil, wine, vanilla and flour mixture. Beat on low for one minute.

Divide the batter between two well-buttered and floured 9-inch cake pans.

Bake for 35 to 40 minutes, or until a toothpick inserted into the center comes out clean.

Cool in pans for 10 minutes on a cooling rack, then invert the cakes onto the racks to finish cooling.

Coconut Cream Frosting

Combine the sour cream, heavy cream, vanilla and the coconut. Add the sugar and stir until well combined.

Arrange one cake layer on a serving plate with strips of wax paper under the edges. Spread on ½ of the frosting mix, then top with the remaining layer.

Frost the top of the cake, but leave the sides unfrosted.

Makes 10 to 12 servings

This recipe as the grand finale for a *Downton Abbey* Birthday tea is perfect. Don't forget the candles!

Birthdays tell others we love them. It's rare if someone has not had birthday parties when they were children, but it happens. All the more reason to celebrate. An afternoon tea party is suitable for many celebrations. It isn't as involved as a dinner party, so it might be just the gala event for many get-togethers. Prepare the food ahead of time, so you will have the luxury of enjoying the event too. Other times to have an afternoon tea include: baby showers, welcoming of a new neighbor, saying good-bye to a friend or neighbor, a bridal shower, a fund raiser, Valentine's Day, Mother's Day, St Patrick's Day, or Easter. It can be very formal, or a buffet style, and can include many guests, or just one. Whatever the reason for hosting an afternoon tea, enjoy!

Birthdays are good for you...the more you have the longer you live.

"Teach us to number our days, that we may gain a heart of wisdom."

Psalm 90:12 NIV

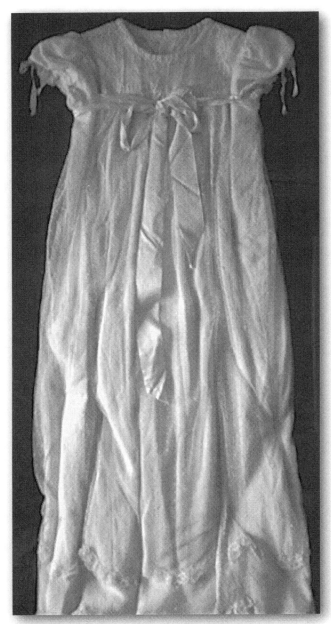

Christening dress photo provided by Karen Webster.

CHAPTER 10

A Christening Tea

• • •

A CHRISTENING. WE DON'T HEAR much about these ceremonies in America, but they are very prevalent in England, as they were in Edwardian times. In fact, according to the magazine Christianity Today, movies and television shows include more scenes of baptisms than weddings. Many people today are not familiar with christenings or baptisms of infants.

There is not a lot of difference between a christening service and a baptismal service. Christening is a traditional English word for the service that welcomes the baby or child into the church family. The local priest performs christenings if a bishop is not available. One or more adults in good standing in the church, who will usually be the godparents, must sponsor a child. The child is baptized with the pouring of holy water over his/her forehead as the priest makes the sign of the cross and prays for the child to be welcomed into the church family. Many use this time to announce the baby's full name.

As the service takes place around the baptismal font, the godparents bear witness to the ceremony and pledge to help the little child grow in the knowledge and love of God.

The birth of a new baby is always cause for celebration. During Edwardian times, the children of upper-class families spent very little time with their parents. Most children had nannies who were responsible for the complete upbringing of the children. It is interesting that the spiritual parts of their young lives would be one of the most planned events in the early years of childhood. Most babies are usually about two to four months old at the time of a christening, so it might be one of the first times family and friends see the new baby.

The christening service takes place at the family's local church, with a luncheon or tea following at the parents' or grandparents' homes. Everyone, including the officiating clergy and his wife, were invited. In a home with servants, such as at *Downton Abbey*, the food and drink were prepared and laid out on the dining room table or sideboard, waiting for the guests' arrival.

Mrs. Patmore, the cook at *Downton Abbey*, is busy at work in the kitchen. She is the one responsible for all the meals, not only for the Crawley family and guests, but the entire staff that runs *Downton Abbey*. Yet she still has time to find the recipes, plan the menus, and then prepare extra events like a christening tea! Oh, that we could all have a Mrs. Patmore in our homes.

The parents or godparents were the hosts of the meal, and most of the food would be white...white sandwiches, white soups, and white cakes. Even the flowers at the service in the church and at home were varying shades of white. The baby wore a white christening gown that most likely had been handed down from earlier generations, and the baby's mother will wear a lovely white or pastel tea dress.

Hats were part of the ensemble of all the women. The party would continue with the traditional small talk the British are so comfortable with, but certain topics were avoided: age, money, politics, religion, and food. It was improper to comment about the food or the decorations in the home, in fact, it was very poor taste to compliment the host of most things.

The guests would have sent their gifts the day before the christening, and were displayed for all to admire. The gifts were intended to be an investment in the baby's life, and were most often silver items such as cups, spoons, bowls, plates, rattles, and even small tea sets. Some people gave money to be deposited into a savings account established to insure a growing investment in the baby's future. I still have the silver christening cup and silver baby spoon given to me by my godparents at my christening many years ago in England.

Downton Abbey doesn't have much to say about religion. There have been overtones of forgiveness and helping the down-and-out, but little mention of church attendance or religion on the series. Lord and Lady Grantham, grandparents for the first time, are upper-class members of the Church of England and are visibly upset that their son-in-law, Tom, an Irish Catholic and former chauffeur to the family, has announced that his and Sybil's baby will be baptized Catholic. *Downton Abbey* viewers were presented with the old-church based conflict that the Church of England (or the Protestant church - churches separate from the Catholic Church: Baptist, Presbyterian, Lutheran, etc.) has a higher status in society than the Catholic Church. The history of the Kings and Queens of England have many times revolved around the church...either the Catholic or Anglican (Church of England) and sometimes with quite head-wobbling effects.

As the family from *Downton Abbey* gathers for the christening at the local Catholic church and not at the Protestant village parish church, Tom asks Lady Mary, the baby's aunt, to be the godmother. I wondered how that was possible, as Mary is a member of the Church of England and the godmother should be of the same faith as the baby who is to be baptized, a Catholic.

I must remember this is television!

Research into the church's role in the early 1900s provided me another look into the class system of that era when I wrote my book *Tea on the Titanic*. Religion was very important to every level of society in those times. On board the *Titanic* all three classes, First, Second, and Third, had religious services during the voyage. I believe it must have been of utmost importance before embarking on such a long trip, that the passengers with children made sure they were baptized.

Baptism has several connotations, and until I had a change in my life I always thought it was my ticket to heaven. I now believe that infant baptism or christening is a dedication of that child into the faith, but the final decision of becoming a Christian is each person's responsibility. Mark 16:16 states: "Believe and be baptized." I have no doubt that the christening service is very important, as it is an agreement between the parents and God. So, while there are continuing debates over these sacraments of the church, whether Catholic or Protestant, all people must come to their own decision about their faith. The Titanic's passenger list included several Roman Catholic priests and Protestant clergy. I can only surmise that as the severity of the condition of the Titanic became more evident to the passengers, the age-old church debate of class status might have disappeared.

Back at *Downton Abbey*, the baby's mother, Sybil, the Grantham's youngest daughter, recently lost her life from complications of childbirth. She had married the family chauffeur, Tom Branson, and they had planned to move to Liverpool, where Tom was to join his brother in a car-repair business. Grandfather Grantham is not happy that his granddaughter would be living in lower standards than befits a member of the *Downton Abbey* clan. The grandparents are faced with the situation of the newly widowed son-in-law, Tom, demanding the baptism in the Catholic Church. Because the family is Protestant, as most of the upper class were during that era and also in England today, the grandparents are very shocked and angry that their granddaughter could be raised a Catholic! But their oldest daughter, Mary, also aunt to the baby, confesses that her younger sister confided in her before she died that she would not oppose having her child being raised a Catholic. With that said, the christening goes on at the local Catholic Church with everyone going back to *Downton Abbey* for the Christening Tea.

Watching that episode provided some interesting insights into the mentality of class structure in that day. Before the service, Grandfather Robert (Lord Grantham) plans on being very uncomfortable at a Catholic service. He recalls going to Mass once when he was in Rome. He feels that he won't know what to do, "all that bobbing up and down – it was more like gymnastics!" But nevertheless, he goes to the service as he knows his daughter, Sybil, would want him there.

My mother was a staunch Anglican (member of the Church of England), so there was never a question as to where our family would attend church. After we resettled in America, the closest faith to the Anglican was the Episcopal church. I grew up in the Episcopal Church with infant christenings, and each child christened, boy or girl, wore a christening outfit, which usually had been worn by other members of their family and passed down. The service was always followed by a meal, most often it was a tea. These were fun and memorable events, as the entire family attended and the children were all glad to be together.

With the recent christening of young Prince George and Princess Charlotte, son and daughter of Prince William and Kate Middleton, there has been a renewed interest in having a child baptized or christened, not only in England but also in the U.S. Both children wore the exact replica of the gown created by Queen Victoria for her oldest daughter's christening in 1841. The gown was remade in 2004 when the Queen realized 163 years of christenings in the same gown was enough! Every royal baby since 1841 has been christened in that gown, made from lovely Honiton lace and ivory satin.

After the service for Prince George at the Chapel Royal in St. James Place, a Christening Tea was held at Clarence House, the London residence of the grandparents, Prince Charles and his wife, Camilla. Slices of Will and Kate's wedding cake were served along with the christening cake and tea.

Little Prince George's sister Princess Charlotte was christened at St. Mary Magdalene Church on the Queen's Sandringham Estate in Norfolk, the same church her grandmother, Princess Diana, was christened in 1961. After Princess Charlotte's service, the Queen invited family and friends to a Christening Tea at Sandringham. While no formal report was given regarding the specific menu for the tea, Darren McGrady, Princess Diana's private chef and former chef to the Royal Family, shared his thoughts. The Royal hand-painted 19th century Meissen china would be used as the guests sip on champagne and tea. The menu included tea sandwiches; cucumber, smoked salmon, egg mayonnaise, and ham. Small scones were served, as they are easier to handle and eat while standing. The Christening Cake might have been the chocolate biscuit cake that William so loves. It was one of the cakes at his and Kate's wedding. The top tier of their wedding cake would be the top of the special cake for Princess Charlotte, a light sponge cake. Most christening cakes also include part of the parent's original wedding cake.

When reading Mr. McGrady's book, *Eating Royally*, I was surprised by his comments about the Queen and scones. "While the Queen insisted on them (scones) as part of her tea, I suspect she didn't actually like scones. I say that because she never, ever, ate them. Instead, at the end of her daily tea, the Queen would take a scone and crumble it onto the floor for the corgis. It seems the dogs quite liked them."

Christenings for the royal family are very important and signify not only the reaffirmation of the family's faith, but in the case of Prince George, the future King, he is also the future Protector of the Faith, and the Supreme Governor of the Church of England. With almost eight million members in the Anglican church, it is an uppermost necessity for the Royal Family to continue on with this tradition. My mother kept a scrapbook of all the important events occurring in the Royal Family for many years, especially the weddings and christenings. As I look over the collection of pictures and newspaper clippings, I realized the importance of those in leadership having a faith that is visible.

My own christening, in England, was in a lovely, old stone Anglican church. I wore an ivory christening gown made of satin with lots of lace and ribbons, passed down from my mother's godchildren, who were thrilled that I was wearing their dress. After the christening, everyone celebrated with a lovely tea at my godparent's home. Because sugar and eggs were difficult to find after World War II, everyone helped with the ingredients for my christening cake. My parent's wedding cake was very small because of the rationing of supplies, so there were no leftovers from their cake to add to my christening cake.

The Queen and Prince Philip were also married about the same time as my parents, and even they were affected by the severe shortage of baking ingredients. Sugar and flour had to be flown in from Australia and South Africa so a cake would be available for the royal wedding.

Many christenings revolve around the cake which most likely is a rich fruitcake covered with marzipan frosting. Today the christening cake is still an important part of the event, evidenced by the wide variety of christening and baptismal cakes advertised. No doubt the cake for the *Downton Abbey* christening was one of Mrs. Patmore's finest creations. As with all significant life-stage events, a christening is a very special day, and the cake is one of the central items for this celebration. At *Downton Abbey*, Mrs. Patmore and Daisy, the kitchen maid, would have been very busy the day before, cooking and baking, with everything ready in the dining room for the arrival of the christening party. Her cake would have been one of her finest creations, with the baby's name and date written across the top of the cake.

Many years ago at my younger brother's christening, the family and members of the christening party went to our home after the service for a traditional tea. My mother played the piano as everyone danced and sang, and the adults enjoyed sipping sherry from small crystal glasses. My mother had her glass sitting on the edge of the piano, and noticed that her glass of sherry was vanishing rather quickly. One of her friends, who was helping with the party and serving the sherry, saw me out of the corner of her eye taking little sips now and then from my mother's glass. I had discovered one of the delights of English entertaining...a little glass of sherry! I do not condone children drinking alcoholic beverages, and this occurrence mandates that adult glasses must remain out of the reach of children.

At *Downton Abbey* the preparations would be very similar, but with Mrs. Patmore and her staff arranging and preparing all the food. She would have made the special christening cake and lots of wonderful sandwiches and scones. Those attending would have arrived in smart dress attire, ladies with hats and men in morning suits. As we saw in the episode with the christening on *Downton Abbey*, everyone was in their finest, especially Tom, the baby's father.

The food was artfully arranged, probably on the sideboard. Mr. Carson served champagne or sherry as the guests admired darling Sybie, before she was whisked away by the nanny to the nursery.

MENU FOR A CHRISTENING TEA

Tea Sandwiches

Cucumber and Cream Cheese
Egg and Cress
Smoked Salmon (Claridges Style)
Spicy Ham

Scones

Royal Scones
Served with Jam and Devonshire Cream

Sweets

Three-layer Christening Cake
Chocolate Biscuit Cake

Teas

Jasmine
Yorkshire Gold
Black Currant

Recipes

Tea Sandwiches

Cucumber and Cream Cheese Sandwiches

The food for this special event should be out of the ordinary. Cucumber sandwiches are a staple at most afternoon teas, and the christening tea most definitely needs some zip! I always love the combination of lemons and cucumber. This recipe caught my eye for something special. I hope you enjoy this delightful addition to the Christening Tea.

4 ounces of softened cream cheese
1 Tablespoon of chopped fresh dill (you may used dried if fresh not available)
Juice and zest of 1 lemon
salt and pepper to taste
Eight slices of thin white bread
1/3 English Hothouse cucumber, sliced very thin and not peeled (place between two layers of paper towels to absorb some of its liquid while preparing the cheese mixture)

Combine the cheese, dill, lemon juice and zest, and salt and pepper. Spread each slice of bread with the cream cheese mixture. Place the cucumber slices on top of the cheese mixture on four slices of bread and top with the four remaining slices of bread. Cut into quarters in desired shape. Cover with a damp paper towel and refrigerate until ready to serve. Plan on each person having two quarters. Makes 16 quarter tea sandwiches.

Egg and Cress Sandwiches

Four boiled and peeled eggs
Six slices of thin white bread (Try to find a square loaf so there is less waste)
3 Tablespoons of mayonnaise, <u>not</u> low fat (I tried, and the result is a flat taste)
1 ½ teaspoon of Dijon mustard
1/3 cup chopped water-cress
Salt and pepper to taste
Softened butter

Mash the eggs so there are no large chunks
Add the mayonnaise, mustard, watercress, salt and pepper until well mixed.
Butter each slice of bread, then place a spoonful of the egg mixture on half of the bread slices.
Top with the remaining bread slices.
Cut the crusts away with a sharp or electric knife into desired shape.
Makes 24 quarter tea sandwiches.

I like to do each type of sandwich in different shapes for variety on the serving tray.

Smoked Salmon (Claridges' Style) Sandwiches

Most salmon tea sandwiches have cream cheese as the spread. When we had after-noon tea at Claridges Hotel in London on one of the tea tours, this sandwich was outstanding. I neglected to ask for the recipe, so here is my rendition of it. I have recently been buying Irish Butter. It is so good and rich and makes a wonderful base for this sandwich.

4 Tablespoons of softened Irish butter
1 Tablespoon chopped fresh dill
1 Tablespoon fresh squeezed lemon juice
8 slices of dense white bread
8 slices of smoked salmon
Very thinly sliced red onion (paper thin)
Salt and pepper to taste

Mix the butter with the dill and lemon juice. Add the salt and pepper and mix well.

Spread the butter mixture onto all 8 slices of bread. Place the smoked salmon on top of 4 slices of bread and then top with a very small amount of the red onion slices, then top with the remaining slices of bread. Trim the crusts with a sharp knife and cut each sandwich into four quarters. Cover with damp paper towel until ready to serve. Makes 16 quarter sandwiches.

Since this is a Christening Tea, all the sandwiches are on white bread in keeping with the theme. If you use these sandwiches for different teas, feel free to use rye or brown bread.

Spicy Ham Sandwiches

This is the time to buy good quality ham, preferably not prepackaged. Have it sliced very thin.

  8 slices bread
  Very thinly sliced ham
  Soft Butter
  Dijon mustard and mayonnaise

Spread butter on both sides of the bread.
Place the ham on one side of the bread and spread the mustard with a small amount of mayonnaise on the other piece of bread. Place the bread slices together, cut off the crusts and cut into desired shapes. Don't forget to cover with a damp towel to keep these tasty sandwiches moist. Makes 16 quarter sandwiches.

SCONES

Royal Scones

I love this recipe. It makes a delicious scone and holds together well. I found this recipe during the time of Prince William and Kate's wedding. I made the scones and my friend, Mary, and I ate these with a cup or two of Earl Grey tea at two in the morning while watching the royal wedding. After the ceremony, we had a glass of champagne and tottled off to bed about 5 a.m.!

    2 cups all-purpose flour, plus more for dusting
    ½ cup sugar
    2 teaspoons baking powder
    ¼ teaspoon salt
    6 Tablespoons unsalted butter, cut into ½-inch pieces
    ¾ cup heavy cream
    1 egg, beaten

For the glaze:

    Powdered sugar, about 1 cup
    1/2 lemon, juiced

Preheat oven to 375° F. Line a baking sheet with parchment paper.

In the bowl of a food processor, pulse together the flour, sugar, baking powder, salt and butter until the mixture resembles a coarse meal. This won't take long, so don't over pulse. Add the egg and slowly add the cream until the mixture comes together.

On a lightly floured counter-top, roll out the dough to about ½-inch thick. Cut the dough into triangles and place on the prepared baking sheet.

Bake for 18 to 20 minutes, or until the edges are golden brown. Transfer the cooked scones onto a wire rack and cool for 30 minutes.

For the glaze:
In a medium bowl, mix together the lemon juice and powdered sugar until smooth. Drizzle the glaze over the baked scones.

Makes about a dozen scones, depending on how big you cut your triangles. Serve with an assortment of jam and clotted cream.

SWEETS

Three Layer Christening Cake

2 ¾ cups sifted cake flour
4 teaspoons baking powder
½ teaspoon salt
4 egg whites
1 ½ cups sugar
¾ cup butter
1 cup milk
1 teaspoon vanilla extract
1 teaspoon almond extract

Preheat oven to 350° F.

Prepare three 8-inch round cake pans by greasing insides and line bottom of pans with parchment paper.

Measure together the sifted cake flour, baking powder, and salt. Sift all together again.

Beat egg whites until foamy, add ½ cup sugar and continue beating until the egg whites form soft peaks.

Beat butter until smooth with electric mixer, then gradually add remaining 1 cup sugar and cream together until light and fluffy. Add the flour mixture alternately with the milk, beating after each addition until smooth. Mix in the vanilla and almond extract, then the egg whites and mix thoroughly into batter. Spread the batter equally between the three cake pans.

Bake for 30 to 35 minutes. Cool cakes in pans for 10 minutes, then remove from pans and transfer to a wire rack top-side down. This will help to flatten the top if it is rounded. When ready to frost, place a little dollop of frosting on the middle of the plate to keep the cake from sliding. Frost the cake on a plate that has wax paper strips covering the edge of the plate. If cake is rounded on top, very carefully slice off rounded part to make a smooth flat top. Put Butter Cream Royal Frosting onto top layer, then add second layer. Repeat process of making a smooth top on 2nd layer. Frost the second layer and place the third layer on top. At this point, place the cake in the refrigerator for 30 minutes, then finish frosting the cake. Add fresh flowers or a topper suitable for a baby's christening.

Butter Cream Royal Frosting

3 cups powdered sugar
1 cup butter
1 teaspoon vanilla extract
1 to 2 tablespoons whipping cream

In a large mixing bowl, mix together sugar and butter, and blend on low speed until well blended, then increase the mixer speed to medium and beat the mixture for another three minutes.

Add vanilla and cream and continue to beat for another minute, adding more cream if needed for spreading consistency.

Chocolate Biscuit Cake

*Almost every newspaper in England, and many in the U.S., have pub-
lished a recipe for this famous, no-bake cake that Prince William chose
as one of the cakes for his wedding. When William was a little boy,
Carolyn Robb, chef for the royal family, began making this cake in the
late 1980's. This recipe calls for McVities digestive biscuits, which can be
found at gourmet markets and World Market.*

3 sticks of butter
¾ cup golden syrup
2/3 cup unsweetened cocoa powder
2/3 cup dark chocolate or chocolate chips
1 teaspoon vanilla
2 – 8 ounce packages Chocolate McVities digestive biscuits
2 ounces chopped pistachios

Frosting:
2 cups dark chocolate chips
2 cups white chocolate chips

Melt the butter with the syrup in a sauce pan.
Remove from heat before it comes to a boil and add the cocoa powder,
dark chocolate and vanilla.
Stir until you have a very smooth mixture.

Crush the biscuits (cookies) in a plastic bag into large pieces.
Stir the crushed pieces and nuts into the chocolate mixture and mix well.

Line the sides and bottom of an 8-inch cake pan with parchment paper or
plastic wrap.

Place the chocolate mixture into the cake pan, making sure the bottom of the pan is pressed down well.

Cool at room temperature, then cover with plastic wrap and place in refrigerator to cool for 2 to 3 hours to set.

When set, remove from pan and place on serving plate.

Melt the dark chocolate chips and spread over entire cake.

Melt the white chocolate chips and drizzle over the top of the cake.

Keeps up to two weeks in an airtight container in the refrigerator for up to two weeks.

Selection of Teas

The heart of most teas is the tea itself. Today we are fortunate to have a wide variety of teas to choose, not like in the early 19th century. Even with all the choices, I think the traditional blends are the most complementary for this special event. I suggest staying with trusted teas that provide a balanced selection for a satisfying flavor for all your guests.

Black Tea Blend
Earl Grey
Darjeeling

All these teas can be served with or without milk. Offer your guests thin sliced lemon and sugar cubes to add for their personal tastes. If using milk, no lemon!

Since a christening is such a special and once in a lifetime event, careful planning is essential. This is a religious milestone for the child and nothing should interfere with the meaning of this special day. Keeping the location of the tea close to the church will insure a stress-free afternoon that will be a meaningful and memorable event for all.

"Bless this child, O Lord, we pray, keep him safe by night and day."

CHAPTER 11

Children's Tea Party

• • •

PLANNING A TEA PARTY FOR children is exciting and fun. The party might be for your child, your niece or nephew, your grandchild, or perhaps a child in the neighborhood, but creating a child's afternoon tea party is a delight for everyone. These parties are a fun way to celebrate special events such as graduations, birthdays, securing the starring role in the school play, or holidays. Remember to include the boys, too!

In *Downton Abbey*, children have a small role in the drama series. Three children have joined the Crawley family, and as the series progresses, their personalities develop and we watch them grow from infants to toddlers. The children are cared for by their nannies. Many viewers of *Downton Abbey* were thrilled when the show brought children into the storylines. They all are adorable, and attach themselves to every viewer. We get glimpses of them when they go to the library and interact with the adults. The oldest granddaughter, Sybbie, is the daughter of Sybil, the youngest daughter of the Crawleys, and Tom Branson, the family's former chauffeur. Sybil lost her life shortly after giving birth to Sybbie from preeclampsia. She is the only baby actually born at *Downton Abbey*. This episode was critical in helping raise awareness to a health issue that still exists today. "These bursts of public attention provide a wonderful opportunity to accurately educate the public about a common, but life-threatening disorder of pregnancy, where the facts could save a life." Preeclampsia Foundation. Preeclampsia is a complication of pregnancy that affects blood pressure and other organ systems. It usually occurs after 20 weeks of pregnancy and is characterized with an increase in blood pressure, many times without the mother even knowing. Symptoms often include dizziness, vision disturbances, rapid increase in weight, headaches and swelling. If left without care, it can cause severe complications and death to the mother and baby. For more information please visit: WWW.Preeclampsia.org.

Later that same year, Lady Mary and Matthew Crawley become the parents of little George…and much to the shock of the viewers, the new father dies in a car accident on the way back to *Downton Abbey* from the hospital. The third child, Marigold, is the daughter of Lady Edith, the middle Crawley daughter, and Michael Gregson, Edith's friend and lover, and is rather a surprise. Mr. Gregson mysteriously disappears in Germany, and Edith gives up her child. For a short time, Marigold lives with a family on a farm near *Downton Abbey*, but after much drama involving the farmer's wife, Lady Edith realizes she needs to raise Marigold herself. After a trip to London, Edith and Marigold come home to Downton Abbey… although not everyone knows that Marigold is Edith's daughter.

Accounts from the Edwardian era suggests that parties for children were important events. Victorian books offer many pictures of children dressed in their finest while attending parties. Today, parents spend hundreds of dollars on lavish birthday parties that might include a multitude of themes. In the Edwardian era, many of the upper class had cooks and servants, with "Mum" just dressing for the event. Most children took tea with their nannies in the nursery, far away from the tea table of their parents. We can be thankful that this is not the protocol today. I have incredible times with my daughter, granddaughters, and grandsons at the tea table, and most of the time they come to tea "dressed to the nines!" They love to choose from my collection of play clothes: party dresses, hats, gloves, and jewelry.

"Cambric tea was hot water and milk with only a taste of tea in it,
But little girls felt grown-up when their
mothers let them drink cambric tea."

LAURA INGALLS WILDER – *THE LONG WINTER*

I suggest including a time for teaching etiquette and table manners at a child's tea. A themed tea also provides opportunities to share historical events and traditions, and introduce social skills. Mrs. Patmore, the cook at *Downton Abbey*, and Daisy, her assistant, would be a lovely pair to help us plan this event. They have a plethora of recipes and ideas, as they spend hours preparing the elegant teas to be enjoyed upstairs.

When preparing for this tea, search your cupboards for Grandmother's teapot and teacups. Other family members might have items you can use. Or rummage through flea markets and antique shops to find just the right teacups or teapot. Always use china teacups and plates. It is amazing how a table set with china and silver can turn little children into very careful diners.

In all my years of having teas with children, not one teacup or saucer was broken. A "magic spell" seems to come over the children, and manners are resplendent (at least for the first thirty minutes). This becomes a wonderful occasion to incorporate quick lessons on everyday etiquette. While writing my book, *First Class Etiquette*, it was apparent that proper etiquette for the tea table is just as appropriate for the dinner table.

It's fun to have a theme for your child's tea party, especially if you include your child in the planning process. Our living room was the scene of an American Doll Tea when one of our granddaughters celebrated her birthday. Her mother is an event planner, so we had very creative decorating and game ideas. The party was a smashing success, enjoyed by the girls and their mothers. Having a theme helps the party planning to fall into place. Since children's parties are so popular, hobby and party stores have an incredible selection of favors, party decorations, invitations, and games. Many items can be ordered on-line, and templates of invitations and decorations can be downloaded. Pinterest.com offers many ideas, recipes, and crafts for children's events.

Planning is the key. You might be a spontaneous person who does everything on a "wing and a prayer," but the majority of us need a blueprint to keep things in order, especially a child's party. Start with a list and keep track of your progress. Don't forget to delegate. Husbands and children can make a big difference in getting things done.

A successful party will have everything ready and organized before the guests arrive. Work backward with your time planner to gauge if you have time to make an extra dessert. Start a party journal. Jot down the date, guests, menu, and any other little tidbits to help you remember the event. It makes planning the next party easier.

KEYS TO A SUCCESSFUL PARTY

* Set the date and time for your tea. Choose a theme. Let your child help plan the tea party.
* Make a guest list. Decide how many children will attend the tea party.
* Purchase or make invitations. Children love to make invitations. When you have decided on a theme, find stickers or a design that will compliment the event. Lots of color and glitter are advised.
* Send the invitations two weeks in advance. You can hand-deliver or mail. It is not proper etiquette to e-mail!
* Make or shop for favors, take-home bags, and place cards.
* Plan the menu and the shopping list.
* Check your linens, serving dishes, silver, centerpieces, etc. Purchase those items needed.
* Choose music to play at the tea party.
* Prepare games and prizes and make nametags.
* Prepare as much of the food as possible in advance.
* Set the table the day before.

For a child's tea party, it is fun to use the same format as a traditional afternoon tea – elegant and a little bit formal. An afternoon tea consists of three courses served mid-afternoon, usually between 2 and 5 p.m.

Small crustless tea sandwiches for the first course, scones with jam and Devonshire cream for the second course, and then the grand finale: tea cakes, tarts, and cookies. If baking the traditional birthday cake, serve in place of the additional sweets. A themed birthday cake is always a big hit for everyone. For younger children, the tea party should not last more than one to one-and-a-half hours. For older children, two hours is the limit.

Select three to four different tea sandwiches. The traditional cucumber sandwich is first on the list. Plan on three or four small quarter sandwiches for each child, depending on the ages and sex. If you are serving three different types of sandwiches for a party of six, one and a half to two slices of bread per person requires 14 to 16 slices. Most loaves of bread have 20 to 22 slices per loaf. Vary the bread, using white, whole wheat, raisin, croissants, pita, and other breads of your choice. Depending on which bread you buy, you will have leftovers. Bread freezes well if double wrapped or placed in a plastic freezer bag. You might have enough bread for your next tea.

Fillings for your sandwiches should include something for everyone. The most popular are peanut butter and jelly, egg salad, cucumber with cream cheese, jam and cream cheese, chicken salad, turkey, and ham and cheese. Always check with parents for food allergies.

Scones are a fun part of a tea party, and children love to take their own jam and Devonshire cream to spread on the scone. Bake small to medium-sized scones, as these are easier for the children to handle.

Just before teatime is a good time to do a mini-etiquette presentation as some (or most) children have never been to a tea party. The following tips can be shared with the children:

ETIQUETTE TIPS

* Place your napkin in your lap. Keep elbows off the table.
* Wait for the hostess to begin eating before you start.
* Use "please" and "thank-you" if you would like more tea or food. No reaching across the table.
* Conversation should be lady-like.
* Hold your teacups with your thumb and index and middle finger. It is not proper etiquette to hold out your pinkie.
* Pay close attention to drinking from the teacup as the tea is hot. No slurping. Take small sips.
* If using milk and/or sugar, use the sugar tongs to remove the sugar cube. No more than one sugar cube for a small cup, or two for a normal sized cup. The milk and sugar go into the cup before the tea. Stir quietly without the spoon clinking the inside of the cup. When finished stirring, place your spoon on the saucer.
* Only an adult will pour the tea.
* To eat your scone, place a spoonful of jam and a spoonful of cream on your plate. Then break off a bite-sized piece and spread on jam and cream for each bite. Another way is to cut the scone in half, and place jam and cream on each half. Do not put the halves together. Take tiny bites.
* Stay seated until the tea party is finished. If you need to use the restroom, quietly excuse yourself and place your napkin next to your plate.

THEMES FOR A CHILD'S TEA PARTY

* American Girl Doll Tea
* Princess Tea
* Teddy Bear Tea
* Red Carpet Tea (Dress Up Tea)
* *Birthday Party Tea (see below)
* Christmas Tea
* Valentines Tea
* Titanic Tea
* Mad Hatter Tea
* Alice in Wonderland Tea
* Garden Tea
* Superman or Starwars Tea
* Ballerina Tea

*When incorporating a birthday-themed tea, the opening of presents for all children is a thrill. It is as important for the birthday child to express his delight when opening a gift-wrapped present, as it is for the giver of the gift to experience the joy of giving.

GAMES FOR A TEA PARTY

Depending on the age of the children, there are some very fun games to play. For children ages five to eight, no more than two games that last less than five minutes each. Everyone likes prizes, so make sure you have enough to go around. With very young children, prizes can be given for participation in the game.

Suggested games:

Five to Eight Years

* Musical Chairs
* Dress Up
* I Spy
* Singing and Dancing
* Red Light-Green Light
* Freeze
* Hide and Seek
* Treasure Hunt
* Memory Games
* Simon Says
* Fashion Show
* Pin the teacup on the saucer
* Ring Toss

Eight to Twelve Years

* Memory Game
* Twenty Questions
* Pitching Pennies
* Fashion Show
* Croquet
* Bingo
* Charades

ITEMS NEEDED FOR YOUR TEA PARTY

* Teacups and saucer
* Small plate
* Silverware: teaspoon, tea knife and fork
* Napkins and tablecloth
* Centerpiece
* Teapot
* Sugar bowl (sugar cubes) and creamer
* Sugar Tongs
* Serving Dishes
* Place cards

MENU FOR A CHILDREN'S TEA PARTY

Sandwiches

Curried Chicken Tea Sandwiches
Cucumber Tea Sandwiches
Peanut Butter and Jam
Egg Salad

Scones

Orange Cranberry Scones
Lemon Blueberry Scones

Mock Devonshire Cream / Jam

Sweets

Easy Berry Tarts
Shortbread Cookies
Jam Roly Poly
Or
A Birthday Cake
Sugar Cubes

Tea

(Choose two)
Cambric Tea
Peach Tea
Strawberry and Kiwi
Decaf English Black Tea

SANDWICHES

Curried Chicken Tea Sandwiches

2 cups white chicken meat (canned is OK)
¼ cup mayonnaise
2 green onions (finely chopped)
¼ cup chopped cashews (*Always check with parents for any allergies.)
½ teaspoon curry powder
Butter (room temperature)
Bread (freeze the loaf of bread first as it will be easier to make the sandwiches)

Cut the chicken into small pieces
Mix together the chicken, mayonnaise, onions, cashews, and curry powder.
Spread the mixture onto buttered bread.
Trim the crusts from the bread and cut the sandwiches into desired shapes.
Keep the sandwiches covered with a damp paper towel until ready to serve.
Makes 16 quarter sandwiches

---

* If nut allergies omit.

Cucumber Tea Sandwiches

½ English Hothouse cucumber
Cream cheese, softened
Dill weed
Bread (freeze the loaf of bread first as it will be easier to make the sandwiches)

Slice the cucumber into very thin slices.

Place the cucumber slices on paper towels to help absorb some of the liquid from the cucumber.

Spread the cream cheese onto the bread slices. (This is a great sandwich to cut into heart shapes. Cut bread with a heart-shaped cookie cutter before making sandwiches.)

Place the cucumber slices on top of the cream cheese on half of the bread slices, overlapping slightly.

Sprinkle the cucumbers lightly with dill weed.

Top with the other bread slices that have been spread with the cream cheese.

Trim the crusts and cut the sandwiches into desired shapes if not using heart shapes.

Makes 16 quarter tea sandwiches.

Egg Salad Sandwiches

6 hard boiled eggs, peeled and chopped fine
1 Tablespoon fine chopped green onion
1/3 cup mayonnaise
1 Tablespoon mustard
1/2 teaspoon salt
1/4 teaspoon pepper

Combine all ingredients well, chill, then spread thinly on buttered slices of bread.
Trim crusts and cut into desired shapes.
Serves 8

Scones

Orange Cranberry Scones

2 cups flour
2 teaspoons sugar
1 teaspoon cream of tartar
1 teaspoon baking soda
1/2 teaspoon salt
1/2 cup butter
3/4 cup orange juice
1/4 cup dried cranberries

Sift together the first 5 ingredients.
Cut the butter into the dry ingredients; add the cranberries, and then stir
in the orange juice. (Less handling of the dough makes fluffier scones.)
Divide dough into 2 portions, then pat into rounds 3/4-inch thick, or cut
into rounds with a floured cookie cutter. Place scones on lightly greased
or parchment -lined baking sheet.
Bake 12 to 15 minutes at 400°F. Makes 10 to 12 scones.
Serve warm with jam and cream - Devonshire cream, clotted cream, or
mock-Devonshire cream.

Lemon Blueberry Scones

These delightful scones don't last long once they are on the table. They can also be made using a small round cookie cutter, just bake for a shorter amount of time.

2 cups flour
½ teaspoon salt
¼ cup sugar
1 Tablespoon baking powder
6 tablespoons butter, cut into pieces
1 cup fresh blueberries (or frozen)
2 large eggs, beaten
¼ cup plain yogurt
1 teaspoon vanilla
1 Tablespoon grated lemon zest
1 teaspoon lemon juice
2 Tablespoons sugar, for sprinkle

Lemon Glaze
½ cup lemon juice
2 cups powdered sugar, sifted
1 Tablespoon unsalted butter
1 Tablespoon lemon zest

Preheat the oven to 375°F.
Lightly grease a baking sheet, or line with parchment paper.
Put the dry ingredients in a bowl and whisk with fork.
Add the butter and using a pastry blender, mix until the mixture is like fine bread crumbs.
Gently mix in the blueberries with the dry ingredients.

Stir together the eggs, yogurt, vanilla, lemon zest, and lemon juice.

Add to the dry ingredients and stir until just until combined.

Transfer the dough to a lightly floured surface and knead the dough gently a few times.

Pat the dough into a circle that is about 8 inches round and about 11/2 inches thick.

Cut into 8 pie-shaped wedges (triangles).

Place the scones on the baking sheet.

Brush the tops of the scones with a little cream or milk and sprinkle with sugar.

Bake for 15 minutes, or until lightly browned.

Remove from the oven, and serve warm with lemon glaze.

Mix the lemon juice with the powdered sugar and microwave for 30 seconds or until the sugar is dissolved.

Stir in the butter and lemon zest and heat for 15 to 20 seconds. Using a whisk, stir the glaze to smooth out any lumps.

Place in the microwave again if needed, and then drizzle the glaze over the scones.

Let it set couple minutes before serving.

Mock Devonshire Cream

Serve the scones with this mock-Devonshire cream.

1 drop yellow food coloring
1 cup heavy whipping cream
¼ cup sour cream

Add the food coloring to the whipping cream
Beat the cream with an electric mixer until very stiff.
Gradually blend in sour cream.
Serve with strawberry or raspberry jam to go with each piece of your scone that you break off.

SWEETS

Easy Berry Tarts

Strawberries, raspberries or blueberries, washed and hulled
Pre-packaged tart shells
Whipped cream or topping

Place berries in tart shells.
Top with whipped cream.

Shortbread Cookies

1 cup butter, softened
1/2 cup sugar
2 cups flour, sifted

Cream together the butter and sugar. Gradually work in flour with your hands until you have a smooth, binding consistency. On a lightly floured surface, knead well to a smooth dough and roll out to ½-inch thick. Cut the dough into fingers, or use a cookie cutter. Place on cookie sheet and prick the top of the cookies with a fork.
Bake at 350°F for about 15 to 20 minutes, until very pale/golden.

Leave for 1 minute to cool, then transfer to a wire rack and sprinkle well with sugar while still warm.
Store in an airtight container, when cool. Don't over-bake; cookies are done when pale/golden. Tops will feel dry.

Jam Roly Poly

An English tradition for children. It is also one of the favorite recipes that the Queen's grandsons (William and Harry) love. A big hit at any tea party.

2 cups self-rising flour
½ cup butter
4 Tablespoons sugar
¼ cup milk
¼ cup water
2/3 cup raspberry jam or preserves
1 Tablespoon milk or cream

Preheat oven to 350° F
Line a cookie sheet with parchment paper

Sift the flour into a bowl and add the butter - cut into small chunks.
Using your fingers or a pastry blender, mix until the dough resembles fine breadcrumbs.
Stir in the sugar. Add the milk and the water with a fork and stir until it is a soft dough.
Turn out onto a lightly floured surface and work together to form a smooth dough.

On a piece of wax paper, roll out the dough into a rectangle, about 5" x 9".

Spread the dough with raspberry jam, leaving about a ½-inch border around the edge.
Roll up lengthwise like a jelly roll and place the roll, seam down, onto the parchment paper on the cookie sheet.

Brush the top with milk or cream and bake for about 30 minutes until golden brown and cooked through.

Let sit for a few minutes, then slice the jelly roll into 8 slices with a serrated knife.

Serve warm as baked, or pour a custard sauce over the top of each slice.

*I use Bird's English Custard as prepared from the instructions on the carton for
the custard sauce.*

Sugar Cubes

These little sugar cubes are fun for your child to help you make. Special candy molds are available to match your theme at hobby stores. These sugar cubes can be decorated with a powdered sugar frosting, or use prepared frosting in a tube.

> 1 cup sugar
> 1 Tablespoon water
> Food coloring
> 1/8 tsp flavoring (optional)
> Plastic candy molds (shallower is better)

1. Place the sugar in a bowl and add the water. Stir until all of the sugar is moistened.

2. Add the food coloring and the flavoring, just a little bit at a time. Stir all together. If a deeper color is desired, add small amounts until desired color is obtained. The sugar mixture should look and feel like moist sand and should clump together when you squeeze it in your hand. If it feels too dry, add a little bit of water until you have the right consistency.

Place the sugar into small plastic candy molds or a sugar-cube mold. Press down into the mold firmly. When finished filling the molds, gently remove any excess sugar from the tops of the molds.

Let the sugar in the molds dry completely before removing from molds. Depending on the weather, this might take several hours or overnight. After removing the shapes from the molds, let them sit at room temperature until they are dry all the way through. The sugar molds should be kept in an airtight container at room temperature. Handle with care.

The sugar cubes can also be decorated with little flowers or other decorations or a powered sugar icing can be piped onto the top.

Tea parties are fun for all ages, and especially for children.

Tea

Cambric Tea

Hot water
Hot milk
1 Tablespoon of prepared Black Tea
1 or 2 sugar cubes

In a teacup or teapot, combine equal parts of water and milk.
Add the tea and sugar cubes, stir and serve.

For several children, make the cambric tea in a teapot and have the child
put the sugar cube(s) into the cups before serving.

In place of tea, children can be served apple juice, punch, milk, or even water. To keep the theme of a tea party, use teapots with teacups and saucers.

CHAPTER 12

English Christmas and Tea

• • •

"I will honour Christmas in my heart, and try to keep it all the year."

CHARLES DICKENS, *A CHRISTMAS CAROL*

CHRISTMAS HOLDS MANY FOND MEMORIES. As a child in the United States, my English mother continued to celebrate Christmas as though we still lived in England. Our tree was placed in front of the living room window on Christmas Eve, and most of the evening was spent decorating the tree and the tabletops in the living room. After dinner, my father read the Christmas story from the Book of Luke in the Bible. My husband and I continue to share the Christmas story on Christmas Eve, even if it is just the two of us.

At midnight, my parents bundled us all up and we went to church for the midnight service. It was the only night of the year when we could stay up so late. The church was aglow with candlelight and the fragrance of evergreens. Fresh-fallen snow would make the roads slippery and kind of scary. We kids loved seeing our breath so frosty while we sang Christmas carols on the way to church. Once we arrived home, we couldn't wait to hang our stockings on the ends of our beds. Christmas morning we found that Father Christmas had left us apples, oranges, nuts and small little treasures. The "real" gifts were under the tree that we opened after breakfast.

"Glory to God in the highest heaven, and on earth
peace to those on whom his favor rests."

Luke 2:14

In England, less emphasis is placed on Christmas Eve, as everything happens on Christmas Day. The Christmas season really starts four weeks before the 25th during the beginning of the church year Advent, a time of preparation and waiting for the birth of Christ. It is a time of hope, although less emphasized in present times, that God will bring peace to our world. The word Christmas means the "day of Christ."

In the hustle and bustle of our daily activities, we have forgotten the real meaning of Christmas. It seems to revolve around the gifts under the tree, the cards in the mail, the many parties and events, which crowd our days. Christmas can be a time of great joy when we celebrate it for the real reason: God showing his great love for us in sending his son, Jesus. The beginning of December, I invite the neighbor ladies and friends for a Candlelight Christmas Tea, to encourage all of us to remember the true meaning of the season.

Christmas at *Downton Abbey* reminds me of the wonderful traditions handed down from one generation to another. Every country has customs that many families keep alive and well. Our family blends my English heritage with my husband's Italian traditions. We celebrate both during the Christmas season, as I make Italian desserts and serve them at my English Christmas teas.

Christmas traditions in England began as far back as the 16th century, when turkeys first appeared on the Christmas table. At that time, the turkey was considered an exotic bird and was only for the rich. Not until the 19th century would it be a staple in many British homes, but only for Christmas dinner. Christmas dinner is usually served in early afternoon and includes trimmings like roasted vegetables, cranberry sauce, Christmas mincemeat pies, plum pudding, and always Brussel sprouts.

Many of the celebrations we observe today had their origins in nineteenth-century England. The Christmas tree was first made popular by Prince Albert, the husband of Queen Victoria. When the Royal Family decorated their Christmas tree in Windsor Castle in 1841, the tradition spread rapidly throughout Britain. The first Christmas card was also mailed in England about the same time.

Our Christmas dinner table always included Christmas crackers, cardboard rolls wrapped in fancy paper and twisted on the ends, with toys and trinkets inside. Each end has a pull-tab, and when pulled makes a firecracker noise. Out pops not only a toy, but also a paper crown and a small card with a riddle or joke. Everyone at the table wears the crown during Christmas dinner. For many years, my aunt in England sent these Christmas crackers in our Christmas package, as they were unavailable in the States. Now they are readily available at most department stores. Christmas Crackers provide a lot of fun at the dinner table, as everyone looks silly with their paper crowns on their heads and shares their joke or riddle.

Mincemeat tarts are also a prominent item at all Christmas celebrations, especially at a Christmas tea. This spicy fruit preserve is traced back to King Henry V's coronation and included meat with nuts, spices, and fruit in lovely pie pastry. In present-day England, meat is rarely added to the mixture.

The crowning glory to any Christmas dinner is the plum pudding or Christmas pudding. It takes several weeks to prepare this dessert. My mother followed the tradition of setting aside the last Sunday before Advent (Stirring Sunday) as the day to begin making our Christmas pudding. Each family member had the opportunity to stir the batter and make a wish before it was set aside to "season." Just before serving, a brandy sauce was poured over the pudding and lit. A flaming dessert! Traditionally, a sixpence would be added to the pudding, and when served, the person who found the coin would have good luck all year. Now many people purchase it on-line at Marks & Spencer in England, and have it shipped. It can also be found in many gourmet markets.

Attending a Christmas play, such as The Nutcracker or Dickens' Christmas Carol, is a tradition that we still observe in our family. It's fun to hear the younger generation ask, "Are we going to see the Nutcracker again this year?" When I was a child, we always listened to the Queen's speech, broadcast in the late afternoon. The Queen has been sending a Christmas Day message every year since becoming Queen in 1952. The tradition of holiday messages began with the Queen's grandfather, King George V, and continued with her father, King George VI. Rarely would an English family miss this message. The Queen typically combines the past year's major events with Her Majesty's personal reflections on Christmas. She never really touches on any political issues, and I doubt unless a major catastrophe happens in England, she won't. The Queen's Christmas message is always released at 3:00 pm in Britain. Before television and the Internet, it didn't reach our radio until quite late on Christmas night or the next morning.

The Spirit of Christmas reflected in the episodes of *Downton Abbey* helps us understand some of the traditions that were observed in such a grand house. Both the upstairs and the downstairs were involved in the decorating and the festivities.

The Christmas tree in Edwardian times had lovely ornaments, mostly glass balls. The elite were able to decorate their trees with many sparkly and bright ornaments, and the average family had strung popcorn or paper chains made by the children. An impressive tree, complete with electric lights, adorns the grand hall at *Downton Abbey*, even though electricity was just becoming available. And most likely, early Christmas tree lights were colored and very expensive. According to historical advertisements, decorating a Christmas tree with electric lights might have cost $2000 in today's dollars. If anyone would have electric lights on their tree, it would have been the Crawleys at *Downton Abbey*. My grandparents used candles on their tree, as did many people in the Victorian and Edwardian era.

Downton Abbey released a charity skit recently at Christmastime. It featured George Clooney as Lord Grantham and was a spoof about the cast. Especially endearing was the fact that all the actors on *Downton Abbey* seemed to be aware of the retelling of certain plot threads, and had a great laugh about it. The parody was taped on the set of *Downton Abbey*, so viewers saw the decorated Christmas tree in the servants' dining hall, and the greenery and candles on their table. Dining downstairs was always very hustle-and-bustle compared to the slow and relaxed pace upstairs. The servants' meals were similar to food eaten today, and the actors do eat and drink on the set of *Downton Abbey* while filming. In interviews, many of them comment on the food, as it usually is under bright lights for may hours and most often not edible. A big, Brown Betty teapot sits on the dining table in the servant's hall, an indication that many cups of tea are consumed during production.

After the Christmas dinner is finished, families typically play games, watch movies, and enjoy their new gifts; but in England, everything stops at 3 p.m. for the Queen's speech. Then, back to the activities until late afternoon, when Christmas tea is served. After the sumptuous mid-day meal, it might seem curious that there could be much room for tea. However, this tea will not be the traditional holiday afternoon tea, but lighter fare. This might include crumpets, a sandwich made with some of the turkey, but always mince pie or mince tarts. Cake might be included, and most likely some of the Christmas pudding that is left over from dinner. The family puts on the kettle, and relax, as the next day is Boxing Day, a national holiday in England.

December 26th is Boxing Day. It's the one day of the year when the staff at *Downton Abbey* would be released from work and return home to their families. The day is celebrated in all parts of the Commonwealth, and has become a national holiday in Britain, with family and friends sharing leftovers. There are several versions of the holiday's origin, all having to do with charity to the poor. Many Anglican churches in England had alms boxes that collected donations during Advent. The box was emptied on Boxing Day and the funds given to the poor. Another version has the aristocracy giving boxes to the servants and letting them have a day off. Either way, it involves giving to the poor. In America, we participate in canned-food drives and the Salvation Army Santas, activities that go back to the founding of such organizations.

Every Christmas, I invite my neighbors and friends in for a Christmas Tea. It is a tradition I started 25 years ago. The invitations are hand-delivered the weekend before Thanksgiving, so I can meet any new ladies before the tea. I have the tea the first week in December. Providing a time of refreshment and friendship before the frenzied month of December begins is the goal. I hope to encourage, not only myself, but also the attendees to reflect on the real meaning of Christmas; not the frenzy of shopping, decorating and cooking, but the time of year to celebrate the birth of Christ. At the tea, we go around the table and share our family traditions. It's also a great time for us to get to know one another more intimately.

Despite living in the same neighborhood, like most modern women, we are all busy and this may be our only time together during the year. Several of the ladies in the community now have coffees and teas during the year to keep us connected. I look forward to unpacking my Christmas teacups, plates, and linens, and experience the excitement of Christmas. Decorating the house and preparing for the tea brings back wonderful memories of Christmas teas over the past 25 years.

During the year I search for little favors I can send home with each guest. The evening or afternoon ends with a friend telling a story with an inspirational message about Christmas. This annual event sets the tone for all of us as we begin our Christmas activities. I have used a *Downton Abbey* theme for the Tea the past few years. It's been a great inspiration to include many of my English traditions that I had forgotten.

The traditional English Afternoon Tea ceremony uses many items from past years that might not be part of your own kitchen utensils and gadgets.

ACCOUTERMENTS NEEDED FOR HOSTING A TEA:

- Tea Kettle – preferably electric
- Teapot
- Tea strainer, tea ball or infuser
- Teacups and saucers
- Small tea plates
- Teaspoons
- Tea or fruit knives
- Dessert forks
- Tea: loose or teabags
- Sugar bowl
- Sugar tongs and sugar cubes
- Milk jug (creamer)
- Serving plates and dishes
- Tablecloth
- Serviettes (tea napkins, 12")
- Serving tray and cloth
- Tea Cozy
- Nice Extras: flowers, candles, music, place cards and favors

After looking at this list, you might realize that you already own many of the items. Don't overlook your china service, as most have teacups and saucers and dessert plates; and some include teapots. I encourage you to use items already in your home, and then add as you are able.

Keys to a Successful Tea:

* Set the date and time for your tea.
* Make a guest list and send out the invitations at least two weeks in advance if possible. (No e-mails!)
* Plan the menu and the shopping list.
* Check your linens, serving dishes, silver, etc.
* Prepare as much of the food as possible in advance.
* Set the table the day before.

CHRISTMAS TEA MENU

Savories and Tea Sandwiches

Crab Tarts
Curried Cashew Chicken Tea Sandwiches
Smoked Salmon Mousse and Cucumber Tea Sandwiches
Stilton and Pear Sandwiches
Deviled Ham Sandwich

Scones

Rhonda's Sour Cream and Vanilla Scones
Sue Dee's Scones

Desserts

Christmas Kisses
Nordie's Lemon and Coconut Bars
Scottish Shortbread
Mince Meat Tarts
Christmas Gingerbread Cookies
Biscotti
Earl Grey Chocolate Truffles

Teas

Christmas Tea
Ginger Mint
English Black

SAVORIES AND TEA SANDWICHES

Crab Tarts

3 ounces frozen crabmeat, thawed.
¼ cup red pepper, finely chopped.
¼ cup green pepper, finely chopped.
¼ cup red onion, finely chopped.
¼ cup celery, finely chopped.
¼ to 1/3 cup mayonnaise
Chopped fresh dill
Salt and pepper

Combine the crab, chopped vegetables and mayonnaise until mixed well, but not soggy.
Add the chopped dill, salt and pepper.
Refrigerate for at least an hour.
A few minutes before serving, put enough crab mixture into each tart shell to fill.
Garnish with fresh dill sprigs.
Makes 30 small tarts about 2-inches in diameter.

You may use frozen piecrust shells or this recipe.

Crust for shells:
2 cups all-purpose flour.
¼ teaspoon salt.
¾ cup of unsalted butter (1½ sticks)
4 Tablespoons iced water.

Put flour and salt into bowl and mix.
Add butter and combine with the flour mixture using a pastry blender until it resembles coarse crumbs.

Add water, a little at a time, until the dough holds together, not too wet or sticky.

Form into a ball, wrap in plastic wrap and refrigerate for at least an hour.

Roll out half the dough on lightly floured board to 1/8 inch thick.

Cut the pasty slightly larger than the tart pans.

Spray the tart pans lightly with cooking spray.

Press the pastry into the pans and cut away excess with your fingers.

Prick the bottom of the tart several times to prevent the tart from puffing up.

Bake at 375°F for 15 minutes, just until lightly tan: do not brown.

Remove the tart shells from the oven, let cool on wire rack for a few minutes, then remove from the pans and continue cooling.

Curried Cashew Chicken Tea Sandwiches

2 cups cooked and chopped chicken breasts (or 1 large can of chicken)
1/4 cup mayonnaise
2 green onions (finely chopped)
1/4 cup chopped cashews
1/2 teaspoon of curry powder
10 slices of sandwich wheat bread

Mix these ingredients well and refrigerate for at least one hour
Spread butter on bread slices
Divide chicken spread evenly between half the bread slices.
Top with remaining bread slices.
Cut off crusts and cut into desired shapes.
Makes 20 tea sandwiches.

Smoked Salmon Mousse and Cucumber Tea Sandwiches

When I first found this recipe I thought it looked like a lot of work, but it is actually quite simple. I have found if you toast and trim the bread before adding the salmon mixture, it can be done in steps. The toast can be warmed slightly, then add the salmon and cucumber before serving.

3 English (hothouse) cucumbers, peeled and thinly sliced
1 lb. smoked salmon, diced
1/4 cup mayonnaise
1/4 cup sour cream
1 Tablespoon chopped fresh dill, plus sprigs for garnish
1 teaspoon freshly ground pepper
3/4 cup chilled heavy cream
20 thin slices pumpernickel bread
8 Tablespoons (1 stick) unsalted butter, melted

Place the cucumber slices between layers of paper towels to remove excess moisture.

Place the smoked salmon in a food processor or blender and process until fairly smooth, 45 to 60 seconds, stopping the machine once or twice to scrape down the sides of the bowl.

Add the mayonnaise and sour cream and process until the mixture is very smooth, 30 to 45 seconds, adding the chopped dill and pepper during the final few seconds. Stop the machine as needed to scrape down the sides of the bowl.

Transfer the salmon mixture to a bowl and nestle it in a larger bowl filled with ice. Cover and refrigerate.

In a chilled bowl, whisk the heavy cream until soft peaks form. Using a rubber spatula, gently fold the whipped cream into the salmon mixture until just blended. Do not over mix or the mousse will be grainy and lose its shape; it should be firm enough to hold its shape when scooped out with a spoon. Nestle the bowl in the ice again and refrigerate.

Preheat a broiler.

Using a pastry brush, lightly brush both sides of the bread slices with melted butter.
Place the slices on a baking sheet and broil, turning once, until golden brown on both sides, about 30 seconds per side.

Place half of the toasts on a work surface and spread about 2 Tbs. of the salmon mousse on each slice.
Arrange the cucumber slices, slightly overlapping, on the mousse and press gently. Top each with one of the remaining toasts.

Using a sharp knife, trim the crusts off the sandwiches.
Cut the sandwiches diagonally into quarters.
Garnish each sandwich with a small dollop of the remaining mousse and a dill sprig.
Arrange on a serving platter and serve immediately.
Makes 40 tea sandwiches

Stilton and Pear Sandwiches

8 slices Honey Whole Wheat Bread (thin sliced)
¼ cup softened butter
1 ripe pear, any variety, sliced thin (sprinkled with lemon juice to prevent browning)
4 ounces Stilton cheese, crumbled

Spread butter on all slices of bread
Place slices of pear on top of the 4 slices of bread, overlapping slightly
Divide cheese evenly on top of pear slices
Top with other slices of bread
Cut off the crusts and cut into desired shapes.

Makes 16 tea sandwiches

Deviled Ham Sandwich

1 small can Deviled Ham or finely minced lean ham
1/4 cup finely chopped green onion
1 Tablespoon Dijon Mustard
8 slices mixed wheat and white bread

Combine all ingredients
Spread ham mixture on 4 of the buttered slices of wheat bread and top
with the other buttered bread slices.
Trim crusts and cut into desired shapes.

Makes 16 tea sandwiches

SCONES

Rhonda's Sour Cream and Vanilla Cream Scones

*I met Rhonda while she and her husband were leading a couple's retreat
my husband and I attended at Forest Home Conference Center in
Southern California. Rhonda and I began to chat and found out we
both loved tea and hospitality. Later in the afternoon, she served these
wonderful scones. Of course, I wanted the recipe! You will enjoy these
delectable scones with or without clotted cream and jam.
(Rhonda Hamner and her husband Curt, have a wonderful ministry
for couples and marriages. www.betweentwotrees.org)*

2 cups flour
1 cup cake flour
2 teaspoons baking powder
1/2 teaspoon baking soda
1/4 teaspoon salt
3/4 cup sugar, plus more for garnish
2 teaspoons finely grated orange zest
3/4 cup butter, cold, cut into small chunks
1 egg, lightly beaten
1/2 teaspoon vanilla extract
3/4 cup buttermilk or orange juice (more if needed)
1 cup dried sour cherries
2 Tablespoons cream

Combine flour and cake flours, baking powder, baking soda, salt, sugar
and zest in large bowl.
Cut-in butter until mixture is grainy and coarse.
Make a well in the center of dry ingredients and stir in egg, vanilla, and
buttermilk or orange juice.

With a fork, lightly bring mixture in toward the center to combine wet and dry ingredients.

When slightly combined, fold in cherries.

Mix lightly with fork to form soft, shaggy mass, adding up to 2 Tablespoons more liquid if needed.

Turn out on a lightly floured counter and knead gently to make a soft dough.

Pat or shape dough into 10"-circle. Cut in quarters, then each quarter in thirds.

Place scones on baking sheet lined with parchment paper.

Brush top with cream and sprinkle with sugar.

Bake at 425° F until golden, about 12 to 15 min.

Makes 12 scones.

Sue Dee's Scones

Sue and I have been "tea sisters" since we first met. Her love of Jesus and her gift of hospitality were contagious. Originally from Zimbabwe Sue and her husband, John, are very involved with helping children in their native country receive education and daily necessities. They take two trips a year to Zimbabwe and allow many people to be part of their ministry by "adopting" children they meet in the orphanages and camps they support. (www.Ebenezer-Ministries.org)
This scone recipe is always one of my favorites for my Christmas Teas.

2 cups self-rising flour
1/4 cup unsalted butter
2 Tablespoons sugar

1 egg, beaten
1/3 cup buttermilk

Place the flour, butter and sugar into a bowl and rub the ingredients together with your fingers, or use a pastry cutter to make the dough the consistency of bread crumbs.

In a separate bowl, mix the egg and buttermilk, then add to the dry ingredients and mix by cutting in with a knife until it comes together into a ball. Be careful to handle as little as possible. Place the dough on a floured surface and pat out into a circle about 3/4 inch thick. Cut into 8 wedges and place on parchment-lined baking sheet. Brush with beaten egg.

Variations: add 1/3 cup currants or craisins, or 1 Tablespoon finely grated lemon rind to dry ingredients.

Bake at 450 ° F for about 12 to 15 minutes.
Serve warm with jam and Devonshire cream.

DESSERTS

When making desserts and sweets for your Christmas Tea, double the recipe. It only takes a few more minutes and you will have lovely gifts for your neighbors or a hostess gift. I usually make bite-size desserts rather than cakes. Like many people, I buy my Christmas Plum Pudding from Marks & Spencers (one of Britain's best loved retailers)!

Christmas Kisses

1 bag Hershey's Christmas Kisses
1/2 cup butter, softened
1 cup sugar
1 1/2 teaspoons vanilla
1 egg
2 cups flour
1/4 teaspoon salt
1/4 teaspoon baking soda
2 Tablespoons milk
Red and green colored sugar

Preheat oven to 350° F
Remove wrappers from candy kisses

Beat butter, sugar, vanilla and eggs in a large bowl until well blended.
Stir together flour, baking soda and salt in a separate bowl.
Alternatively add the milk and flour mixture to the butter mixture and beat until well blended.

Shape the dough into 1- inch balls.
Roll the balls in the colored sugar.
Place on ungreased baking sheet.

Bake for 8 to 10 minutes until the edges are lightly browned and the cookie is set.

Remove from oven and cool for a few minutes.

Press a candy piece into the center of each cookie.

Remove the cookies to a wire rack and cool completely.

3 dozen cookies

Nordie's Lemon and Coconut Bars

My friend Mary and I were having lunch at Nordstrom's Café and finished our meal with these delicious lemon bars. They were not your usual lemon bar, so Mary asked our server if we could have the recipe. Several minutes later, we left the café with a copy of the recipe. We have since learned that Nordstroms does not give out recipes, so don't tell them where you got this!

Crust:

  2 cups flour
  3/4 cup sugar
  1 teaspoon salt
  2 cups coconut – flaked, toasted, and chilled
  4 ounces butter, cubed

Filling:

  3 cups sugar
  8 eggs
  3/4 cup fresh lemon juice
  Zest from two lemons
  1 Tablespoon flour
  1 1/2 teaspoon baking powder
  1/4 teaspoon salt

Topping:

  2 cups whipping cream
  8 ounces mascarpone cheese
  1 Tablespoon vanilla
  1/2 cup powdered sugar
  3 cups coconut
  Garnish – 1/4 thin slice lemon for each bar

Using a food processor, pulse the butter and the dry ingredients until a grainy dough forms.

Press the dough into a parchment-lined and buttered jelly roll pan.

Bake for 10 minutes at 350° F. or until light brown.

Place the filling ingredients into the food processor and blend until well mixed. Pour the filling over the hot crust and bake at 350° F. until slightly set and just browned – 25 to 30 minutes. Freeze to set firmly and chill.

To make the whipped topping, whip the cream until stiff peaks form. Add the vanilla and powdered sugar. Fold in the mascarpone cheese and spread over the chilled filing. Top with the coconut and freeze. Unmold and cut into 2" by 3" bars. Garnish with lemon slices.

This makes almost 60 pieces. I suggest you cut the recipe in half for your afternoon tea.

Mince Meat Tarts

Christmas just wouldn't be Christmas without mincemeat tarts. I start looking for the jars of mince around the first part of November. Most grocery stores now sell mincemeat. If you don't use the whole jar, freeze until ready to use. I used to make large pies, but these little tarts are so easy to make and serve.

2 cups flour
½ teaspoon salt
1 Tablespoon sugar
1 cup butter
2 to 3 Tablespoons iced water

1 jar mincemeat filling

Mini muffin tins

Combine the flour, salt, and sugar and combine with a fork
Add the butter with a pastry blender until the mixture resembles coarse meal.
Add the water slowly until the dough just holds together when pinched. If necessary, add more water.

Put the dough onto a floured surface and pat it into a ball. Divide the dough in half and form into two balls.
Wrap each ball in plastic wrap and refrigerate for 30 minutes.

Roll out the dough between two sheets of wax paper until about 1/8 inch thick.
Cut into rounds that are slightly bigger than the muffin tins.
Place the rounds into the muffin tins and form to fit the tin.

Place one teaspoon of mincemeat filling into each dough filled tin (about 2/3 full).

Top with a pastry star that you have cut from the dough.

Brush the tops with a little egg wash (1 egg beaten with a couple teaspoons of water) and sprinkle with sugar.

Bake at 400° F for 12 to 15 minutes until lightly browned.

Cool on a wire rack then dust with powdered sugar before serving.

These freeze well.

Makes 24 – 2 inch tarts.

Scottish Shortbread

I have been involved in several clubs for Brits, and it is always a delight to share recipes.
My British friend Catherine gave me this recipe…one of the best!

2/3 cup unsalted butter, softened
1/4 cup powdered sugar
1 1/2 Tablespoons sugar
Pinch of salt
1 1/2 cups all-purpose flour

Preheat the oven to 300° F.
Lightly grease cookie sheet with butter.

With a fork, mix the sugars into the softened butter until thoroughly blended.
Gradually stir the flour and salt into the butter mixture, until thoroughly blended.
If the dough is too dry, sprinkle a few drops of water over it, being careful not to over-moisten.

Roll out the mixture until it is about 1/4-inch thick.
Cut with cookie cutters and gently place onto prepared sheet.
Bake on the middle rack for about 45 minutes. Set your timer for 35 minutes.
When lightly golden around edges, remove from oven and cool on pan for 5 minutes, then remove and place on wire cooling rack.

Christmas Gingerbread Cookies

These wonderful cookies have been part of the Christmas season for hundreds of years. Their fragrant aroma will get you in the Christmas spirit when you start baking.

1 stick unsalted butter, room temperature
½ cup brown sugar
1/3 cup molasses
1 egg
2 teaspoons orange zest

2 ½ cups flour
2 teaspoons ground ginger
1 ½ teaspoon ground cinnamon
¼ teaspoon ground nutmeg
¼ teaspoon ground cloves
½ teaspoon baking soda
¼ teaspoon salt

In a small bowl, mix together the flour, ginger, cinnamon, nutmeg, cloves, baking powder, and salt.

Using an electric mixer, cream the butter and brown sugar together until smooth.
Add in the molasses, orange zest, and egg and combine well.
Keep mixer speed on low and gradually add in the dry ingredients until a soft dough forms.
Divide dough into thirds and shape into round disks about 2 inches thick.
Wrap dough in floured plastic wrap and refrigerate for 1 to 2 hours.

Preheat oven to 350° F.
Remove dough from refrigerator and place on floured surface.

Roll out the dough until it is about ¼ inch thick. Use enough flour so the dough doesn't stick.

Use a gingerbread man cookie-cutter to cut out dough.

Place cookies on parchment-lined cookie sheets and place in freezer for 15 minutes.

Remove from freezer and bake for 8 to 10 minutes until firm and edges are just beginning to brown.

Cool on cookie sheet until cool.

Transfer to a wire rack.

Pipe a border of white icing around the edge of the cookies using a pastry tip on a pastry bag.

Decorate with two cinnamon candies on a dot of frosting for buttons. Tie a thin red ribbon around the neck of the gingerbread man.

Icing:
  ½ cup confectioners' sugar
  1 Tablespoon milk
  1 teaspoon light corn syrup

Using a wire whisk mix all ingredients together until smooth. Place in a pastry bag and pipe cookies.

If too thick, add more milk, if too thin, more sugar.

Biscotti

At Christmas, we blend my English heritage with my husband's Italian traditions. Italians love these anise-flavored cookies that many people think of having with coffee or hot chocolate, but they are always enjoyed at tea time, too. This recipe makes almost 100 cookies, so it is a great gift item – place in a clear poly bag and tie with Christmas ribbon.

3 ½ cups flour
1 teaspoon baking powder
¾ teaspoon salt
6 large eggs and one egg white for glazing
2 cups sugar
2 teaspoons vanilla
2 Tablespoons liqueur (Disaronno)
1 Tablespoon anise
4 cups coarsely chopped whole almonds

Adjust oven rack to lower middle and upper positions.
Preheat oven to 325° F.
Line two large baking sheets with parchment paper

In a medium bowl, whisk flour, baking powder, and salt.
Beat eggs and sugar with an electric mixer until light and foamy for about 2 minutes.
Beat in vanilla, liqueur, and anise.
Add dry ingredients and nuts until blended thoroughly.
Cover and chill dough for at least an hour.

On a lightly floured board divide dough into four portions.
Roll dough into 4 flat loaves 15 inches long and 2 inches wide.
Place the loaves on the baking sheets, 2 to a sheet, with space between the loaves.

Brush each loaf with the beaten egg white and sprinkle with sugar.
Bake until pale golden brown, and just beginning to crack, about 15 minutes.

Remove from oven and let cool 20 to 25 minutes.
Cut each log diagonally ½-inch thick with a serrated knife. Log should still be warm.
Lay slices on cut sides on baking sheet and keep close together.
Return to oven and bake at 300° F for 20 minutes until lightly toasted.
Cool on wire racks.
Store in airtight container

Earl Grey Chocolate Truffles

This recipe will delight any chocolate lover. I used to think truffles were super complicated to make, but this recipe is rather simple. I have tried it with several different kinds of chocolate with yummy results!

1 cup heavy cream
8 ounces semi-sweet chocolate, chopped into small pieces
3 Earl Grey tea bags
1 teaspoon vanilla
Cocoa powder for coating
Finely chopped almonds

Place cream into a small saucepan and bring to a simmer.
Add tea bags and cover for 5 minutes.
Remove the tea bags, and bring the cream to a boil again.
Immediately stir the cream into the chocolate and whisk until smooth.
Add vanilla, then cover and refrigerate for 2 to 3 hours.
Using a scoop, make small balls that you roll in the palm of your hand.
Roll in the cocoa and place on a parchment-lined baking sheet.
Chill, then place in a covered container

CHAPTER 13

Molly Brown Comes to Tea

• • •

THE FATEFUL SINKING OF THE *Titanic* launched Margaret Brown to international fame almost overnight. She is nearly as famous as the magnificent ship itself; one rarely talks about one without the other. The opening scene in season one of *Downtown Abbey*, takes place in April, 1912, when the newspapers' top story reveals that the heir to the Crawley fortune has perished on the Titanic. Margaret "Molly" Brown, (she was never called Molly in her lifetime) was among the first-class passengers on the *Titanic*. She had spent the social season in Europe, and was called home suddenly, as her grandson was ill. The first available ship she could book passage on was the *Titanic*.

She likely would have been a guest at *Downtown Abbey* before returning to America. Adding a little twist to the series plot, it might be that Margaret came to visit the Crawleys when she heard her friend Martha Levinson, mother of Cora Crawley, Countess of Grantham, was a guest at *Downtown Abbey*. (Actually, she didn't appear in *Downtown Abbey* until season three, but this is television!) Being close to the same age, and in the same social circles, it would be shocking to have two women with very liberal attitudes visiting the aristocratic household at the same time. Mr. Carson would be overly shocked and wonder if the British class system could survive. Both women were very forward thinking and freely offered their perspective on almost anything, whether solicited or not. The two of them were a breath of fresh air!

Several years ago, at the 147th birthday celebration for Mrs. Brown in Denver, I met her great-granddaughter, Helen Benziger. We immediately hit if off and have now become great friends. Helen had no idea she was related to Margaret Brown until she was 13 years old, awhen her mother took her to see the film, The Unsinkable Molly Brown. Helen's desire is to have her great-grandmother recognized for the remarkable woman she was, not how she was portrayed in the Broadway musical or movie, as a "loose woman who danced on bartops!"

Mrs. Brown was a most remarkable woman. As a teenager, she helped with the family income by working in a factory, and dreamed of moving west and making an impact on her community. At the age of eighteen Margaret and her brother Daniel moved to the mining town of Leadville, Colorado. She met James Joseph Brown, a mining engineer from Pennsylvania, at a church picnic. J.J., as he was called, was thirteen years older than Margaret. She always planned on marrying for money, but said on many occasions that she "married J.J. for love." They married and had two children, Lawrence and Helen.

In 1891, after several years of marriage, the Browns became "overnight millionaires." J.J. had been involved with the Little Johnny Mine in Leadville, Colorado, when they struck gold. The mine became one of the biggest and richest in Colorado. The Browns moved to Denver and bought a house that remained their family home for almost 50 years. Their house once served as the Governor's Mansion and is now a museum. The Molly Brown House has been restored and is the site of many teas and special events.

Margaret was a women's rights advocate with a commitment to social reform, and even added politics to her platform when she ran twice unsuccessfully for the U.S. Senate. The juvenile court system was one of her most prized projects and she was very influential in advocating new laws that separated juveniles from adult inmates. She also spearheaded a campaign to raise funds for the beautiful Catholic Cathedral of Immaculate Conception, just a few blocks from her home in Denver.

Molly Brown was one of the lucky ones who survived the sinking of the Titanic. She worked tirelessly to get as many women and children into the lifeboats and was finally "pushed" into the lifeboat herself, just as it was being lowered. When the rescue ship Carpathia arrived in New York, the unsinkable Mrs. Brown was in the spotlight for her bravery and subsequent fund raising efforts. More than $10,000 was collected from the Carpathia's passengers and crew to help defray costs of the survivors.

When reporters were permitted to interview those on the Carpathia, they asked her to give an account of how Molly had survived. She replied, "Typical Brown luck, we're unsinkable!" She actively pursued an interest in the stage, and lived the life of a new woman of the 1920s, free, liberated, and self-sufficient. During this stage of her life, she learned five languages, traveled extensively, and continued her advocacy of women's rights.

I have found the spirit of Molly Brown in the life of her great-granddaughter, Helen. We have talked often about how history repeats itself and is perpetuated in future generations. Knowing Helen, I feel I have touched history in a very tangible way. As Helen and I grow in our friendship, we are thankful for the friends who introduced us. Tea was the common bond!

Margaret loved to entertain, and I am sure as a guest at *Downton Abbey*, she would have loved having tea with Cora, Violet, and Martha! Can you imagine the conversation? The old protocol of not discussing money, sex, or politics flew out the window. In its place, the opportunity to have conversations that were beyond gossip prevailed. All three women were well versed in social and cultural civility, and might have brought some much-needed "worldly-minded" comments to the tea table.

Having a Molly Brown Tea is a great joy and I hope you, the reader, will love the recipes that Helen has approved and Margaret would have loved.

UNSINKABLE MOLLY BROWN TEA MENU

Tea Sandwiches

English Cucumber
Smoked Scottish Salmon
Coronation Chicken
Cheese and Nut Pinwheels

Scones

Raspberry Cream Scones
Raspberry Preserves and Devonshire cream

Homemade Lemon Clotted Cream

Sweets

Mini Apple Spice Cakes
Lemon Fruit Tarts
Chocolate Shortbread Bites

Teas

Earl Grey
Raspberry Cream
Darjeeling

Molly Brown Tea Recipes

Sandwiches

English Cucumber Tea Sandwiches

1 English hothouse cucumber
Butter - room temperature
Thin sliced white bread
Dill weed

Peel and slice an English hothouse cucumber as thin as possible.
Place in a colander and sprinkle with a small amount of white vinegar and salt.
Place a plate and large unopened can on top to weigh it down.
Leave cucumbers to drain for at least 30 minutes.
Place cucumber on paper towels and press out any remaining liquid.
Spread white bread with softened butter and cover half the slices with cucumber.
Sprinkle lightly with dill.
Top with second slice of buttered bread, trim crusts and cut into desired shapes.
Optional: use cream cheese instead of butter.

Smoked Scottish Salmon Sandwiches

8 slices rye or pumpernickel bread
1/4 cup butter, softened
4 ounces smoked salmon slices
2 ounce watercress (stems removed)
Pepper and dill weed

Spread butter over slices of bread.
Arrange slices of salmon on top of buttered bread
Season with pepper and dill weed
Place watercress on top of salmon slices
Place remainder of bread on top of watercress
Trim crusts from bread and cut into four quarters

Coronation Chicken Sandwiches

In 1953 when Queen Elizabeth II was crowned queen of the British Empire, the entire country celebrated. This salad was made in her honor for the Coronation Luncheon. There are many variations, but I think you will enjoy this one.

2 cups cooked and chopped chicken
3-4 stalks of celery, chopped
3 ounces dried apricots, chopped
1 ounce slivered almonds
1/4 jar mango or peach chutney (cut-up large bits of fruit)
1 teaspoon curry powder
3 finely chopped green onions
Salt and pepper to taste
Enough mayonnaise to hold salad together

Place all ingredients in bowl, mix well and refrigerate for several hours.
Spread on white or whole wheat buttered bread.

Cut off crusts and cut into triangles.
Keep covered until ready to serve.
This sandwich is usually a favorite, so make plenty.
(Two quarters of each sandwich per person are average)

Cheese and Nut Pinwheels

½ cup chopped and roasted pecans or walnuts
1/3 cup finely chopped pimentos
4 ounces cream cheese, softened
1/3 cup mayonnaise
¼ cup chopped green onion
butter
6 slices of nutty wheat bread

Combine first five ingredients and mix well.
Remove crusts from bread and roll the slices with a rolling pin to flatten.
Spread bread slices with butter.
Divide the cream cheese mixture equally between the 6 slices of bread.
Spread the cheese mixture onto the bread slices and roll up jellyroll style.
Wrap in plastic wrap and refrigerate one hour.
Slice each roll into 4 to 6 slices. Keep covered until ready to serve.

Makes 24 to 36 pinwheel sandwiches.

Scones

Raspberry Cream Scones

*When I first met Helen, she introduced me to the Molly Brown Tea
that she had blended and packaged. It was a Raspberry and Cream
Tea and I asked why she had chosen that blend. Her reply was, "Well,
I know her favorite thing for breakfast was raspberries and cream, so
I thought what a wonderful way to start the day!" Our family loves
raspberries and I usually have some frozen in my freezer, they are what
you need for this recipe.*

2-½ cups flour
¼ cup sugar
2-½ teaspoons baking powder
Zest from one lemon
1/2 teaspoon salt
1 stick of unsalted butter
1 cup heavy whipping cream
1 cup frozen raspberries

Preheat oven to 375° F
Line a baking sheet with parchment paper

Combine flour, sugar, baking powder, zest, and salt with a wire whip.
Using a pastry blender, cut the butter into the dry flour mixture until it
resembles coarse crumbs.
Pour the cream into the mixture and stir gently until most of flour is
mixed in.

Turn the dough out onto a floured surface and gently knead until the
dough holds together.
Add more flour to the surface area and roll dough into a 8" x 10" rectangle.

Place the frozen raspberries onto half the dough, then roll the half without raspberries over the half with the berries.

Gently press the top layer into the bottom layer.

Using a 2 inch round cookie cutter dipped in flour and cut out as many as possible and place them carefully on the baking sheet.

Using remaining dough, gently press dough together and flatten and cut out the remaining scones.

Brush the tops of the scones with cream and sprinkle with sugar.

Bake for about 15 minutes or until scones are golden brown.

Cool for several minutes before moving to a plate and serving.

Serve warm with jam and Devonshire cream.

SWEETS

Lemon Fruit Tarts

1 box of refrigerated pie crusts (2 crusts) at room temperature

Filling
   1 4-ounce box instant lemon pie filling
   1 cup cold milk
   1 Tablespoon grated lemon zest
   Whipped cream for topping
   1 pint fresh raspberries
   Mint leaves for garnish

On a lightly floured surface, unroll piecrusts. Using 3-inch round cutter, cut 14 to 16 circles from dough. Press each dough circle into ungreased muffin tins. Prick the bottom with a fork several times. Bake, for 5 to 7 minutes or until golden brown. Cool completely on a wire rack (about 15 minutes).

Mix the milk, lemon zest and pie filling mix with an electric mixer or whip until well blended. Spoon pudding mix into cooled tart shells. Top with a dollop of whipped cream, a raspberry, and two mint leaves.

Chocolate Shortbread Bites

1 cup flour
1/3 cup butter at room temperature
1/4 cup powdered sugar
2 eggs
1 ounce unsweetened chocolate, melted in microwave on defrost, cooled
1 cup sugar
1/2 teaspoon baking powder
1/4 teaspoon salt
1 teaspoon vanilla

Combine the flour, butter, and powdered sugar until mixed well.
Press into an 8-inch square baking dish and bake at 350° F for 20 minutes.
Beat remaining ingredients together until fluffy.
Pour this mixture over the hot cookie crust and bake for another 20 to 25 minutes or until set.
Cool and cut into squares.
Can be made ahead and kept in an airtight container. Makes 16.

Mini Apple Spice Cakes

1-¼ cups coconut oil
2 cups lightly packed brown sugar
3 large eggs
3 cups all-purpose flour
1 teaspoon baking soda
1 teaspoon baking powder
½ teaspoon salt
2 teaspoons cinnamon
½ teaspoon cardamom
2 teaspoons vanilla
3 Tablespoons buttermilk
3 cups peeled and chopped apples (can use combination of different apples)
1 cup chopped pecans
Powdered sugar for topping

Preheat oven to 350° F.

Grease and flour a mini-Bundt pan, or spray with baking spray with flour.
Beat the oil and sugar with an electric mixer until creamy.
Add the eggs, one at a time, beating after adding each egg.
In a large separate bowl, with a wire whip, mix together the flour, baking soda, baking powder, and spices.
With the mixer on low speed, add the dry ingredients, one cup at a time, then the buttermilk and vanilla.
Fold in the apples and the nuts. Batter will be thick.
Fill each of the mini-Bundt pans ½ full.

Bake until a toothpick inserted into the center comes out clean…about 20 minutes. Transfer the cake pan to a wire rack and cool for 15 minutes.

Unmold the cakes, place cakes flat sides down on a wire rack and cool completely.

Before serving, top the cakes with sifted powdered sugar.

> *"There are two ways of spreading light - to be the*
> *candle or the mirror that reflects it."*
>
> - EDITH WHARTON

CHAPTER 14

Tea on the Titanic

• • •

ON THE MORNING OF APRIL 15, 1912, news comes to *Downton Abbey* in the early edition of the newspaper that the Titanic has hit an iceberg and sunk, with more than 1500 passengers missing and presumed dead.

The very first episode of *Downton Abbey* opens with this scene. I can hardly believe it! I have just completed writing a book about the *Titanic*, *Tea on the Titanic*, and spent many hours on research and writing, and had no idea that *Downton Abbey* had any connection to the *Titanic*. But, wait! It's 1912. Of course, this was the same era. I felt I was in very familiar territory and that was all it took to get me hooked on this drama. I knew where I would be every Sunday evening, watching *Downton Abbey* in my cozy chair with a cup of tea.

As the program proceeds, later in the day Lord Grantham receives an urgent telegram notifying him that his nephew Patrick, and Patrick's father James, are among the passengers lost at sea. They were the heirs to *Downton Abbey*. Patrick was going to wed Mary, the oldest daughter, so the property would automatically pass through him, as the Crawleys only had daughters. This marriage would keep *Downton Abbey* in the family. Now everything was at risk. Would the Crawley family be able to remain in this prestigious estate? A lot of history has led to this point. Mary's mother, Lady Cora

Grantham, is a rich American who came to England to "buy" a title. It was a legal transaction called an entail, money for a title. That is where the Titanic involvement ends, but where the Edwardian era continues.

The Titanic was not supposed to sink. After all, she had been called "Unsinkable" by almost everyone. She was the most beautiful, and the largest, ship ever built; expense was not spared by the owners. Constructed to impress and attract the world's most elite travelers, the *Titanic's* maiden and only voyage had some of the world's richest and most famous people aboard: John Jacob Astor and his pregnant 19-year-old wife Madeleine, who had left America for a few months to escape public controversy certain to surround his choice of a child bride; Margaret "Molly" Brown, the Colorado millionairess, who needed to rush home to be with her sick grandson; Sir Cosmos Duff-Gordon and his wife, the famous British fashion designer Lady Lucille Duff-Gordon, creator of the "Lucille Dress Salons" in London, Paris and New York; George and Eleanor Widener of the Philadelphia Railway System and their 27-year-old son, Harry; popular writer Jacques Futrelle and his wife, Lily May; Walter Douglas, director of The Quaker Oats Company, and his wife Mary Helen; and Major Archie Butt, the ship's most famous bachelor, Military Aide to President William Howard Taft and, formerly, to President Theodore Roosevelt. Quite an impressive list of passengers.

A British ship, such as the *Titanic*, served afternoon tea around 4 p.m. First- and second-class passengers experienced tea similar to the Crawley family's at *Downton Abbey*. The third-class passengers had "high tea" or their evening meal in the lower decks, similar to the servants in *Downton Abbey*, who ate in the servants lounge downstairs.

Those who enjoyed lavish lifestyles, without concern for the cost, comprised the first-class passengers of this opulent floating hotel. The *Titanic*, as grand as any five-star hotel, certainly satisfied their obsession with all things luxurious, especially fine dining. Afternoon tea would have been one of the prized social events of the day, with many of Lady Duff-Gordon's fabulous "tea-dresses" worn by the socialites. The ladies on board would have dressed in the latest Paris and London gowns, and hats adorned with lace, pearls, feathers, ribbons and satin.

As they gathered for afternoon tea in the sitting rooms of their suites, or the Verandah, Palm Court or Café Parisie, they sipped tea and enjoyed dainty tea foods. Their conversation most likely centered on fashion, the theater, or the next social event they would attend when back in New York. The passengers on this ship all had high expectations of their journey across the Atlantic. The first- and second-class passengers expected a carefree and enjoyable vacation, third-class passengers beheld the promise of a new way of life in America.

The demise of the *Titanic* is a story that has been told many times in movies, books, and newspapers. Much research has been done and continues to be a fascinating area of study for many people. The discovery of the wreck of the *Titanic* in 1987 confirmed many theories, and thousands of artifacts have been brought to the surface. I had the privilege of meeting Robert Ballard, who is best known for his discovery of the *Titanic*, at a recent appearance at the University of Colorado. He shared his experience of going down two-and-a-half miles to the wreckage of the *Titanic*, where he also took pictures. Opportunities such as this always give me new insight and interest in the ship and her passengers.

> *"...all of these very, very different types of people were having to face the same disaster and suddenly they were united."*

> - JULIAN FELLOWES

Museums and exhibitions all over the world display everything from large portions of the hull to unbroken bone-china teapots and teacups. It's sobering to realize that these articles were on a ship that should not have sunk.

My interest in the *Titanic* began when I was a little girl on a trip home to England with my parents. We traveled from New York City to Southampton by ocean liner on the S.S. United States, the fastest ship in the world at that time. My mother and I were enjoying afternoon tea in the lounge, when she remarked, "This must have been like it was on the

Titanic; all the china and silver, lovely tea sandwiches and pastries, and having a view of the ocean – tea at sea." I didn't know what she meant: the *Titanic*. My mother knew quite a lot about that fateful voyage and shared the story with me. That afternoon is where it all began; "tea at sea" - my interest and subsequent love of the Edwardian era, and especially the *Titanic*.

I imagined Molly Brown having tea at *Downton Abbey*, and it was just as easy to visualize the Crawley family traveling first-class on the *Titanic*. The mingling of the Americans and the British on board proved comfortable for all. In that timeframe, formality was expected. Everyone knew what to wear to certain events, and to follow protocol. Tea time was one of the highlights of the day. The female passengers changed from their day dresses to tea frocks, complete as to undergarments and hats and gloves. The Edwardian ladies changed their clothes, on the average, of six times a day. Can you imagine the amount of luggage for a transatlantic voyage?

Recreating afternoon tea on the *Titanic* is an opportunity to relive the splendor and the romance of that era of transatlantic travel. It wasn't cruising, but a crossing. Preparation of tea on the Titanic was by experienced chefs and bakers, but we can create similar menus using similar recipes… with the ease of the many convenience foods available today.

I have the feeling that if we had to prepare food as they did during the Edwardian era, we all would want Mrs. Patmore to move into our homes. I hope you will have some fun recreating the recipes that I have used at many of my afternoon teas.

1ˢᵀ Class Afternoon Titanic Tea Menu

Tea Sandwiches

Chicken Tarragon
R.M.S. Salmon
Egg and Capers
White Star Cucumber
Olympic Cheddar

Scones

The Ritz Scones
Cherry Chocolate Scones

Desserts

Pavlova with Strawberries and Cream
White Star Mini Bundt Chocolate Raspberry Cakes
Cinnamon Stars

Teas

English Breakfast
Earl Grey
Titanic Tea
Oolong Tea

RECIPES FOR TITANIC TEA

TEA SANDWICHES

Chicken Tarragon Sandwiches

2 chicken breasts, cooked and chopped fine
2/3 cups chopped celery
1 small shallot, finely chopped
½ cup dried cranberries
½ cup chopped toasted pecans
1 Tablespoon finely chopped fresh tarragon leaves
1/3 cup sour cream
¼ cup mayonnaise
Salt and pepper to taste

White sandwich bread – 10 slices

Combine chicken with the rest of the ingredients and add salt and pepper.
Chill for several hours or overnight.
Butter one side of bread slices
Divide chicken between 5 of the bread slices.
Top with remaining bread slices.
Trim crusts with electric knife into triangles.
Keep covered with damp paper towels until ready to serve.

Makes 20 tea sandwiches

R.M.S. Salmon

4 ounces smoked salmon, flaked
¼ cup chopped pecans
1 teaspoon finely chopped chives
¼ cup mayonnaise
Finely chopped fresh parsley
1 loaf marble rye bread

Mix salmon, pecans, chives and mayonnaise well.
Spread 8 slices of bread with softened butter.
Divide the salmon mixture and spread evenly between 4 slices of bread.
Top with other buttered 4 slices of bread.
Cut sandwiches into star shapes with a star-shaped cookie cutter. If cookie cutter does not cut completely through, use a sharp knife to complete the cutting.
Lightly spread edges of sandwiches with butter and sprinkle the chopped parsley over the butter.

Makes 16 star sandwiches.

Egg and Capers

This sandwich takes the traditional egg salad and puts a fresh and elegant twist on an old favorite recipe.

6 eggs, boiled and cooled
1/3 cup finely chopped red onion
2 Tablespoons chopped capers
¼ cup mayonnaise
1 teaspoon Dijon mustard
Salt and pepper to taste

6 slices white bread
6 slices pumpernickel bread

Finely chop eggs
Mix the mayonnaise and mustard together.
Combine the eggs, onion, and capers.
Add mayonnaise mixture to eggs and mix well.
Add salt and pepper.

Butter the bread slices.
Place the egg mixture on the white bread.
Spread egg mixture just barely to the edge of the slices.
Top with the pumpernickel slices.
Using a round cookie cutter, cut sandwiches into rounds.
Use a sharp knife if cookie cutter did not go all the way though the bottom slice of bread.
Keep covered until ready to serve.

Makes 24 round sandwiches.

White Star Cucumber

I English hot-house cucumber
Softened cream cheese
6 slices white sandwich bread
Garnish for top: small mint leaves or parsley

Wash cucumber, but do not peel.
Using a vegetable peeler, slice long strips from the cucumber and place the cucumber strips on triple-thickness paper towels.
Sprinkle with a very small amount of salt.
This will help draw out some of the moisture from the cucumber.
Spread cream cheese onto the bread slices.
Lay cucumber strips across the bread, overlapping, until each slice is covered.
Using a sharp knife, trim off the crusts and cut each slice into 3 equal strips.
Sprinkle with a little black pepper and a very small amount of sea salt.
Garnish each sandwich with mint or parsley.

These sandwiches should not be made the night before the tea, as the bread can become soggy.

Makes 18 Sandwiches

Olympic Cheddar

The Olympic was the sister ship to the Titanic and was almost identical, with very small differences. The Olympic continued to sail until 1935 and was nicknamed "Old Reliable." She was sold for salvage and scrap and many of her luxurious fittings were removed and can be found, even today, in hotels, restaurants, and cruise ships. On a recent cruise, I dined "one ship inside of another," as the décor for the dining room featured the original paneling from the historic RMS Olympic.

1 cup sharp cheddar cheese, shredded
1/3 cup finely shredded carrots
1 Tablespoon finely chopped onion
3 strips well-cooked bacon, drained and crumbled.
½ cup mayonnaise
Sandwich wheat bread – 8 slices
Unsalted butter, softened.

Combine first five ingredients, and refrigerate for at least one hour.
Spread butter onto bread slices, divide and spread the cheese mixture between 4 slices. Top with the other 4 slices.
Trim crusts with an electric knife and cut into triangles.

Makes 16 sandwiches

SCONES

The Ritz Scones

There must have been many recipes used from the Ritz Hotel in London on the Titanic, as the famous hotel's top chef served on the Titanic. I can't imagine that the Ritz Hotel in London would ever give out their recipes, but many years ago, I copied this one from a cooking column in the L.A. Times, but it was for the Ritz Carlton Hotel in California!

1/4 cup unsalted butter, softened
1 cup powdered sugar
4 cups pastry flour
2 Tablespoons baking powder
1 egg
1 1/4 cups milk
Pinch salt

1/4 cup dried apricots, chopped
1/4 cup raisins

Cream together the butter and powdered sugar.
Add the pastry flour, baking powder, egg, milk, and salt.
Mix the egg and milk together and stir into the butter and sugar mixture.
Mix just enough to blend. Do not over-mix
Add the apricots and raisins.

Place dough onto lightly floured surface and pat out to a 1" high circle. Cut with floured round cutter, and place on parchment-lined cooking sheet.

Bake at 400° F for 8 to 10 minutes.

Serve warm with jam and Devonshire cream.

If made ahead, warm for 5 minutes covered with foil at 250° F.

Makes 15 scones.

Cherry Chocolate Scones

I think these scones are very modern and would not have been baked by either the baker on the Titanic nor even Mrs. Patmore. Chocolate in scones? They are very tasty and many women have told me they now make these scones on a regular basis. Enjoy!

2 cups flour
¼ cup sugar
1 Tablespoon baking powder
½ teaspoon salt
½ cup frozen butter, grated
1 cup heavy whipping cream
¼ cup dried cherries, dusted with flour and chopped
2 ounces mini semisweet chocolate chips

Preheat oven to 450° F.
Stir together flour, sugar, baking powder, and salt.
Cut the butter into the flour mixture with a pastry blender until it resembles coarse crumbs
Add 3/4 cups of whipping cream, cherries, and chocolate.
Stir until just blended and moist. If too dry, add a little more cream.

Turn dough out onto a floured surface and pat dough into an 8" round.
Cut into 8 wedge shaped pieces, like a pie.
Place the wedges 2 inches apart on a parchment-lined cookie sheet.
Brush tops of scones with remaining cream and sprinkle with a small amount of sugar.

Bake for 12 to 14 minutes until golden brown.
Serve with cherry preserves or jam, and Devonshire cream.
Makes 8 scones

SWEETS

Pavlova with Strawberries and Cream

This very elegant dessert was named after the Russian ballerina Anna Pavlova, after she toured Australia and New Zealand in 1926. It is said of her, "She does not dance; she soars as though on wings." Her namesake, sometimes called a meringue, is light and airy, with a touch of finesse.

3 large egg whites – room temperature
1/4 teaspoon cream of tartar
1/4 teaspoon salt
1 teaspoon vanilla extract
1/2 cup sugar

Preheat oven to 275°F
Line cookie sheet with parchment paper.
Draw eight 3- to 4 - inch circles onto the parchment paper.

Make sure all the utensils used for making this dessert are clean and free of any oils.

In a large bowl, beat the egg whites with an electric mixer. Start with a low speed and increase slowly until at high speed.
Gradually add cream of Tartar and salt until egg whites begin to mound.
Continue beating at high speed and add vanilla and sugar, sprinkling in one tablespoon of sugar at a time, making sure the sugar is completely dissolved after each addition.
Egg whites should stand in stiff and glossy peaks when the beaters are lifted, after approximately 4 to 5 minutes.

Spoon meringue mixture inside the circles on the parchment paper. With the back of a spoon, shape and spread meringue into a "nest" with the sides about 1-1/2 inch high.

Bake meringue shells about 1 to 1-1/4 hours.
Check on meringues at least once during baking.
Turn off the oven and allow the meringue to remain in the oven for one hour to dry out. Transfer the meringue shells to a wire rack and cool completely.

The meringue can be made a day ahead and stored in an airtight container. Do not fill until ready to serve.

Filling:
1 pint heavy whipping cream, whipped until stiff peaks form.
Fresh strawberries washed and hulled. Any fresh fruit that is season can be used in place of the strawberries. Be creative.

Just before serving, place the meringue on serving plates and fill with whipped cream. Top with strawberries or other fresh fruit.

White Star Mini Bundt Chocolate Raspberry Cakes

Greasing a bundt pan is important to make sure the cake does not stick to the pan. Either use a brush with melted butter and then flour, or use a baking spray. After flouring, shake the extra flour out. Make sure all the little nooks and crannies are covered ! You could also make these little gems with a chocolate cake mix. Just don't tell the Chef or Mrs. Patmore.

2 ½ cups flour
1 cup of baking cocoa
1 teaspoon salt
2 ½ teaspoons baking soda
1 ¼ cup unsalted butter, softened
2 cups sugar
3 eggs
2 teaspoons vanilla
1 ½ cup buttermilk
1 cup fresh raspberries

Powdered sugar
Whipping cream

Preheat oven to 350° F

Butter well and flour 12 mini-bundt pans
Combine the flour, cocoa, salt and baking soda.
Beat the butter and sugar with an electric mixer until it is pale and fluffy.
Add the eggs, one at a time, mixing after the addition of each egg.
Stir in the vanilla.
Add dry ingredients in 3 additions, alternating with the buttermilk.

Spoon the batter into each of the mini-bundt pans, filling just 2/3 full.
Mash the raspberries a little and add a heaping teaspoon to each cake.
Bake 20 to 25 minutes or until a toothpick inserted comes out clean.

Let cool, then turn out onto a cooling rack.
Sprinkle with powdered sugar before serving and add a dollop of whipped cream, if desired.

Top each cake with a raspberry.

Cinnamon Stars

½ cup firmly packed brown sugar
¼ cup butter
1 Tablespoon cold water
1 cup plus 2 Tablespoons flour
2 Tablespoons cornstarch
1 teaspoon cinnamon
1/8 teaspoon salt
¼ cup sliced almonds

Beat sugar and butter with electric mixer until well blended.
Add water and beat well.
Combine flour, cornstarch, cinnamon and salt.
Add dry ingredients to butter mixture, beating until well blended.
Gently press dough into a round disk and wrap in plastic wrap.
Place in freezer for 30 minutes.

Preheat oven to 375°F.

Remove dough from plastic wrap.
Roll dough out to a thin 1/6- inch thickness on a floured board.
Cut with a 2 inch star-shaped cookie cutter.
Place cookies on a parchment-lined baking sheet and sprinkle lightly with sugar, then with almonds, pressing into the dough gently.
Bake at 375° F for 8 minutes or until cookie edges are lightly browned.
Remove from oven and cool 1 minute on baking pan, then place cookies on wire racks to cool.

Makes 4 dozen

Making the Perfect Cup of Tea

• • •

CHOOSE GOOD QUALITY LOOSE-LEAF TEA.

Fill the tea kettle with fresh cold water. (Previously boiled water has lost its oxygen).

Bring the water to a boil.

Warm the teapot with hot water, then pour it out when the water in kettle has come to a boil. The tea will brew better and stay hot longer.

Measure tea leaves into the teapot or tea infuser, and pour the boiling water over the tea leaves.

Let the tea steep for 3 to 5 minutes. Green and Oolong teas require less time with water that has just come to a boil.

(Longer brewing time will not make the tea stronger, just bitter)

Pour the tea into a teacup using a tea strainer. If using an infuser, remove before pouring tea.

If you are using milk in your tea, only use milk, no cream, half and half or coffee flavorings. Milk and sugar go into the cup first as milk dissolves better in a hot liquid.

Tea is best brewed in a china or ceramic teapot.

Don't scrub out a teapot after use. It will become seasoned by just rinsing the tea pot with hot water.

Storing Tea

• • •

KEEP TEA IN A TIGHTLY covered ceramic or tin container.
Keep away from sunlight and heat.
Do not refrigerate or freeze.
Tea will stay fresh for 18 to 24 months if stored properly.

Tea for a Crowd

• • •

Tea Concentrate

Measure 1/4 to 1/3 cup of loose-leaf tea into a large 6-cup teapot.
Bring 1 quart water to a boil.
Pour boiling water over the tea leaves.
Steep for 3 to 5 minutes
Strain the tea and divide the concentrate between four 6-cup teapots.
Fill teapots with boiling water and serve.
The concentrate may be made ahead of time and kept refrigerated for several hours.

.

Sandwich Making Tips

• • •

Use thin or sandwich bread...a mix of wheat and white.

Check with your bakery if they make Pullman loaves.

Make your own bread, even colored. Add food coloring with the liquid, before the mixing.

One sandwich loaf of bread will make about 40 tea sandwiches.

Make each kind of sandwich the same shape. Such as: egg salad - squares, the chicken - triangles, the cucumber - fingers, etc.

Freeze bread before making sandwiches. This prevents the bread from tearing and easier to cut when finished.

Seal bread with butter or cream cheese to prevent soggy sandwiches.

Keep fillings for sandwiches moderately applied, not too thick.

Cut off the crusts and into shapes with an electric knife.

After making sandwiches, place them in a waxed paper-lined plastic container

Cover sandwiches with a damp paper towel or lettuce leaves.

Cover entire container with plastic wrap before sealing.

Keep sandwiches refrigerated until use.

Do not put sandwiches into the freezer.

Keep a damp paper towel, large lettuce leaves or damp tea towel over the sandwiches until served.

Recipe Index

• • •

Savories

Beans on Toast, 30
Cornish Pasty, 31
Cottage Pie, 38
Crab Tarts, 176
Pie Crust, 33
Sausage Rolls, 34
Scotch Eggs, 35
Scottish Stovies, 37
Toad in the Hole, 36
Tomato Tartlets, 108

Sandwiches

Cheese and Nut Pinwheels, 206
Chelsea Curry Chicken, 90
Chicken Tarragon, 220
Coronation Chicken, 205
Cranberry, Turkey, and Arugula, 109
Cucumber and Cream Cheese, 129
Cucumber Children's Tea Sandwich, 154
Curried Cashew Chicken, 178

Curried Chicken, 153
Curried Egg, 110
Deviled Ham, 182
Egg and Capers, 222
Egg and Cress, 130
Egg Mayonnaise, 87
Egg Salad, 155
English Cucumber, 203
Olympic Cheddar, 224
Open-face Cucumber, 111
R.M.S. Salmon, 221
Roast Beef and Horseradish, 86
Smoked Salmon, 89
Smoked Salmon, Claridge's style, 131
Smoked Salmon Mousse and Cucumber, 179
Smoked Scottish Salmon, 204
Spicy Ham, 132
Stilton and Pear, 181
Triple Decker Cucumber, 88
White Star Cucumber, 223

Scones and Breads

Beer Bread, 42
Cheese Scones, 40
Cherry Chocolate Scones, 227
Cinnamon Circle Scones, 112
Cranberry Scones with Buttermilk glaze, 113
Crumpets, 44
Honey Scones, 41
Irish Potato Scones, 39
Irish Soda Bread, 43
Lemon Classic Scone, 91
Lemon Blueberry Scones, 157

Norfolk Lavender Scones, 92
Orange Cranberry Scones, 156
Raspberry Cream Scones, 207
Rhonda's Sour Cream and Vanilla Scones, 183
Royal Scones, 133
Sue Dee's Scones, 185
The Ritz Scones, 225

Clotted Cream, Devonshire Cream, Frostings, Misc.

Butter-Cream Royal Frosting, 136
Clotted Cream or Devonshire Cream, 93
Coconut Cream Frosting, 118
Microwave Lemon Curd, 99
Mock Devonshire Cream, 159
Sugar Cubes, 163
White Chocolate Dipped Strawberries, 115

Cakes

Cherished Coconut Wine Cake, 117
Chocolate Biscuit Cake, 137
Coconut Cream Frosting, 118
Jam Roly Poly, 161
Lemon Coconut Poppy Seed Cake, 46
Three-layer Christening Cake, 135
Victoria Sponge Cake with Madeira Cream, 100
White Star Mini Bundt Chocolate Raspberry Cakes, 230
Mini Apple Spice Cakes, 211

Cookies and Bars

Biscotti, 195
Chocolate Shortbread Bites, 210

Christmas Gingerbread Cookies, 193
Christmas Kisses, 186
Cinnamon Stars, 232
Madeleines, 95
Nordie's Lemon and Coconut Bars, 188
Scottish Shortbread, 192
Shortbread Cookies, 160

Pies/Pie Crusts
Fruit Tarts, 97
Mince Meat Tarts, 190
Pastry Shell, 97
Sue's Pie Crust, 33

Puddings/Desserts/Tarts

British Bread and Butter Pudding, 49
    Sauce for Bread and Butter Pudding, 50
Easy Berry Tarts, 160
English Trifle, 45
Fruit Tarts, 97
Lemon Fruit Tarts, 209
Mince Meat Tarts, 190
Pavlova with Strawberries and Cream, 228
Rachel's Sticky Toffee Pudding, 47
Sauce for Bread and Butter Pudding, 50
White Chocolate Dipped Strawberries, 115

Truffles

Earl Grey Chocolate Truffles, 197
No-bake Chocolate Truffles, 116

Illustrations

• • •

CHARLES DANA GIBSON (1867-1944) is the artist whose illustrations grace these pages. He was the perfect chronicler of the Edwardian and wartime years. His Gibson Girl drawings were popular in America and England. Twice Gibson lived in Great Britain to study and paint; and his sister-in-law was Lady Astor. His distinctive pen work and social themes influenced a generation of illustrators. His work appeared in magazines, calendars, and on hundreds of post card designs in England.

Gibson's pictorial observations of the social life of his era were no less popular in the land of the *Titanic* and of the homes that inspired Illustrations by Charles Dana Gibson. The creator of the Gibson Girl, the cartoonist (1867-1944) flourished during the same period spanned by the series *Downton Abbey*. The drawings in this book originally appeared in the old *Life* magazine in America and *Pictorial Humor* in Great Britain. They are from the collection of prominent historian and publisher Rick Marschall and are copyright Rosebud Archives (www.rosebudarchives.com). They may not be reproduced without permission except for purposes of review.

AUTHOR PHOTO BY: RICH VOSSLER (RichVossler.com) is a prominent wedding, portrait, and lifestyle photographer, in Denver, Colorado.

Highclere Castle Photo by: Carol Spurway Carol lives in Ely, Cambridgeshire, England, and has a passion for photography.

She works in the computer software industry and loves spending her free time visiting homes and gardens around England. She believes she captures memories with her camera. You may find more of Carol's work at: www.flickr.com/photos/cspurway

Printed in Great
Britain
by Amazon